T0008393

Praise for
The Hedgewitch's Little Book of Lunar Magic

"*Lunar Magic* is an enchanting well of knowledge that reaches to our ancient roots and reconnects us with our ancestors through lunar symbolism before opening a magical gateway to developing a rich practice by the silvery light of the moon! The spells within this guide are beautiful, melodious, and are able to be customized to suit the individual. By emphasizing the right time within the lunar cycle to set certain intentions, this book empowers one's practice with the force of Earth's only natural satellite shining like a beacon in the sky. The seeker may find that the magic within is not only swift but also effective!"

—Amber Criste, musician and intuitive

"This 'little book' is a source of inspiration to integrate the Moon in a concrete way into our spiritual practice. Tudorbeth offers not only valuable information but a wide variety of practical exercises that undoubtedly help us cultivate our relationship with the 'pearl' of the sky. I loved it. It has so many details and info that surprised me. The content is like a dessert that you want to keep eating,"

—Dhraoi, druid and witch

THE
Hedgewitch's
LITTLE BOOK OF
Lunar Magic

© Sarah Coyne

ABOUT THE AUTHOR

Tudorbeth is the principal of the British College of Witch-craft and Wizardry and teaches courses on witchcraft. She is the author of numerous books, including *A Spellbook for the Seasons* (Eddison Books, 2019). Tudorbeth is a hereditary practitioner; her great grandmother was a well-known tea reader in Ireland while her Welsh great grandmother was a healer and wise woman.

THE
Hedgewitch's
LITTLE BOOK OF

Lunar
Magic

TUDORBETH

Llewellyn Publications
Woodbury, MN

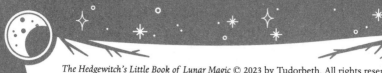

The Hedgewitch's Little Book of Lunar Magic © 2023 by Tudorbeth. All rights reserved. No part of this book may be used or reproduced in any manner whatsoever, including internet usage, without written permission from Llewellyn Publications, except in the case of brief quotations embodied in critical articles and reviews.

FIRST EDITION
First Printing, 2023

Book design by Donna Burch-Brown
Cover design by Shannon McKuhen
Interior art by the Llewellyn Art Department

Llewellyn Publications is a registered trademark of Llewellyn Worldwide Ltd.

Library of Congress Cataloging-in-Publication Data (Pending)
ISBN: 978-0-7387-7560-9

Llewellyn Worldwide Ltd. does not participate in, endorse, or have any authority or responsibility concerning private business transactions between our authors and the public.

All mail addressed to the author is forwarded but the publisher cannot, unless specifically instructed by the author, give out an address or phone number.

Any internet references contained in this work are current at publication time, but the publisher cannot guarantee that a specific location will continue to be maintained. Please refer to the publisher's website for links to authors' websites and other sources.

Llewellyn Publications
A Division of Llewellyn Worldwide Ltd.
2143 Wooddale Drive
Woodbury, MN 55125-2989
www.llewellyn.com

Printed in China

OTHER BOOKS BY TUDORBETH

The Hedgewitch's Little Book of Spells, Charms & Brews

The Hedgewitch's Little Book of Seasonal Magic

The Hedgewitch's Little Book of Flower Spells

The Hedgewitch's Little Book of Crystal Magic

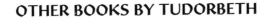

Llewellyn's 2023 Witches' Spell-A-Day Almanac
(Contributor)

Llewellyn's 2024 Magical Almanac
(Contributor)

Llewellyn's 2024 Witches' Companion
(Contributor)

Dedication

Dedicated to those who come alive at night; let us all meet under the wild moon to dance and be merry.

Blessed be sisters and brothers,
To all our friends and lovers,
We are all one underneath the moon's bower,
Living free within the moon's power.

Disclaimer

The material contained in this book is for information purposes only. It is not intended to be a medical guide or a manual for self-treatment. This book is sold with the understanding that the publisher and author are not liable for the misconception, misinterpretation, or misuse of any information provided. If you have a medical problem, please seek professional medical advice and assistance.

Contents

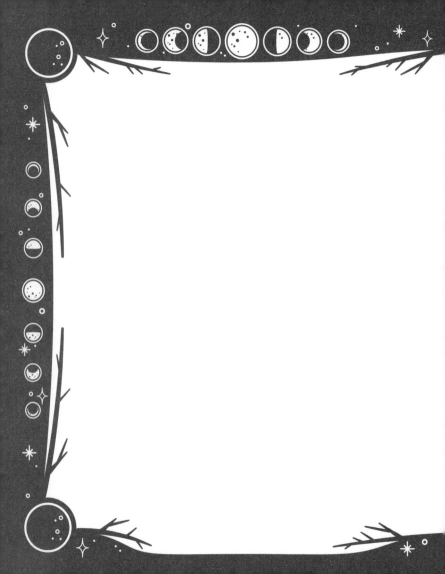

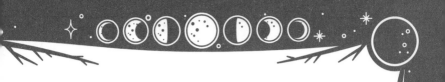

Introduction

Human beings have been fascinated with the moon since we first gazed upon this bright glowing orb in the night sky. As we grew in our learning, the moon took on various personas, including the goddesses Diana, Selene, Artemis, Hecate, Isis, and Cerridwen, to name but a few. The moon is often gendered as female. She is our wise mother, staring down at us while her consort or brother, the sun, rules the day.

Not all planets have moons, and we are exceptionally lucky to have one (and such a beautiful one). The moon rules our tides and, some would argue, our emotions, as the human body is made up of over 60 percent fluid. Ancient Greek philosopher Aristotle believed just as the moon ruled

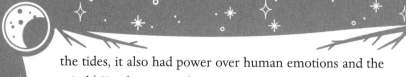

the tides, it also had power over human emotions and the mind.[1] Yet the moon also acts as a shield against meteors and other external forces that could potentially be fateful for the earth.[2]

The moon also gives light on dark nights, and for many thousands of years, it was used as the marker of time, with the whole world following a lunar calendar. Time, tide, light, and protection—our moon is a welcome presence in our skies.

Our moon became a main presence in religions and belief systems around the world, such as in Hinduism or Buddhism, with the moon as an enduring symbol of enlightenment. In Islam, the symbol of the crescent moon represents the religion. In many Asian cultures, festivals of the moon still hold a central part of the calendar, such as in

1. E. M. Coles and Donna J. Cooke, "Lunacy—The Relation of Lunar Phases to Mental Ill-Health," *Canadian Psychiatric Association Journal* 22, no. 3 (April 1978): 149–152.
2. NASA, "Overview: Earth's Moon," NASA Solar System Exploration, last updated January 9, 2023, https://solarsystem.nasa.gov.

China or Japan with the annual Moon Festival celebrated in autumn.

The moon found her way into every aspect of our lives, including the new emerging medical science of the day, as in the sixteenth-century belief that the waxing phases of the moon enhanced the benefits of bloodletting.[3] In addition, for thousands of years, gardeners and farmers have planted and harvested according to the phases of the moon, making sure it was the perfect time to sow or gather the crops.

There is one religion that emerged with the moon as a central figure, and that is witchcraft, nature craft, the Craft, or whatever name you wish to call the belief in magic, spells, incantations, and ritual with nature at its core. The moon emerges on the horizon and stays for as long as there are those of us who will dance under her.

The folklore myths and legends stem from a time when many could not write, and so practices were passed along the

3. Royal Museums Greenwich, "Can the Moon Really Affect Our Health?" Royal Museums Greenwich, accessed January 10, 2023, https://www.rmg.co.uk/stories/topics/can-moon-affect-our-health-behaviour.

generations via word of mouth. As artists began to depict witches, often they were underneath a moon, and usually a full moon.[4] The stereotypical symbols of the witch, such as those depicted in Hans Baldung Grien's (1484–1545) *The Witches' Sabbath*, indicate a prevalence of nude, elderly female forms cavorting with demons, conjuring spells, and flying by full moonlight on broomsticks.[5]

Many of our references concerning the moon and witches stem from that time when both were revered but above all feared, resulting in what many witches now refer to as the burning times. Thus, it is hard to believe that the moon, which is so powerful, innocent, and beautiful, would become our greatest threat. In trials and forced, tortured statements, dancing under a moon for a sabbath, which became known as the Esbat, became a central part of the

---

4. Like in Albrecht Durer's *The Four Witches* (1497) and Hans Baldung Grien's *Bewitched Groom* (1544).

5. Hans Baldung Grien, *The Witches' Sabbath*, 1510, colour woodcut from two blocks, The British Museum.

trials, and subsequently has become part of the stereotypical image of a witch.[6]

However, this book is not about those days, and whatever is written in the past concerning our history we should take with a pinch of salt, preferably even moon salt (see page 108). This book is about tuning in to the moon and utilizing every aspect of her and her power in our lives, days, and nights.

As a hereditary practitioner of the Craft, the moon holds a special place in my practice and heart. When I was young, I knew when the full moon would be without even looking at a lunar chart or calendar; my body would let me know each month, and if you listen to your body, you can know, too. You can learn to live in harmony with the moon and prepare yourself for her most powerful times—such as a full moon, an eclipse, or an equinox—by keeping a moon journal.

---

6. Anne Llewellyn Barstow, "On Studying Witchcraft as Women's History: A Historiography of the European Witch Persecutions," *Journal of Feminist Studies in Religion* 4, no. 2 (Fall 1988): 7–19.

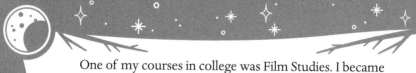

One of my courses in college was Film Studies. I became fascinated with early films, especially George Melies's masterpiece *Le Voyage dans la Lune* (A Trip to the Moon). This brilliant piece of early cinema tells the story of a group of astronomers landing on the moon and is inspired by Jules Verne's 1865 novel *From the Earth to the Moon* and its sequel *Around the Moon*. What struck me most was how personal and interactive Monsieur Melies made the moon, giving it a persona and a face. This connection was something I had grown up with—that the moon was not a dead satellite, a piece of rock that just lit up our night sky; it was indeed a being with its own life force that we can learn to live and work in harmony with. This book is a result of all those years I have worked, honoured, and respected the moon.

In this book, you will learn to create spells, brews, and charms that have been performed or charged under the watchful gaze of the moon. I will describe harnessing the moon's energy for certain magical practices, such as when to create a magical resource or the best time to store herbs.

In the chapter on moon months, I will share both the northern and southern hemisphere names for the moon

6

and include spells and magical practices that can be used for both hemispheres. We might be under different skies, but we all share the same moon. In fact, the moon and her power bring us together as we realise how connected we actually are under her watchful gaze.

As with any of my spells and magical practices, these are only suggestions. Always feel free to change them to suit your circumstances and pocket. Magic is about taking ownership of where you are at and who you are as, ultimately, all magic stems from you.

Enjoy this book on moon magic in which I have tried to give every piece of knowledge and information I have been taught about Our Lady of the Night.

Blessed be, merry meet, and merry part,
We all have moon magic in our hearts.

Tudorbeth

Moon Facts

It is hard to realise how far away the moon really is; if we were to walk to the moon from the earth, it would take at least nine and a half years. And if we were to walk around the moon, it would take us almost a whole year to do so, as our moon is one quarter the size of the earth.

The science behind our moon highlights the fascinating power it has over our earth and how closely we are related. There are many theories about the age of the moon, and they are connected to how the earth came about. The main view is that the moon is about four and a half billion years old after the earth was struck by a cosmic body roughly the same size as Mars. This idea is called the Giant Impact Theory as the resulting debris from the mass collision formed the moon.[7] Therefore, in some strange way, the moon is not necessarily our mother, but rather our child born from one massive explosion billions of years ago.

EARTH-MOON DANCE

The moon is 238,855 miles from the earth.[8] This distance from the earth changes every year as the moon is actually moving gradually away from us at a rate of 1.5 inches each year.[9] This is because of the complex relationship between the earth and moon called gravity. The moon's gravity pulls on the earth and the earth's gravity pulls on the moon. However, the earth's gravity is far greater, which causes the rotation of both to slow; it also makes the moon retreat and move away from the earth. This rotation has slowed to the point that the moon no longer rotates relative to the earth,

7. W. K. Hartman and D. R. Davis, "Satellite-Sized Planetesimals and Lunar Origin," *Icarus* 24 (1975): 504–514, https://doi.org/10.1016/0019-1035(75)90070-6.

8. Royal Museums Greenwich, "How Far Away Is the Moon?" Royal Museums Greenwich, accessed January 10, 2023, https://www.rmg.co.uk/stories/topics/how-far-away-moon.

9. Rick Stroud, *The Book of the Moon* (New York: Doubleday, 2009).

and that is why we always see the same face of the moon, no matter where we are in the world or at what season or time of year.

The Tides

The moon governs our tides because of that gravitational pull between the earth and its satellite. This complex interaction between the earth and the moon is played out on a timely basis day after day as we watch the tides retreat and return. The side of the earth facing the moon bulges toward it, so water also bulges toward the moon. At the same time, on the opposite side of the earth, the water is pulled away from the moon. The sun also has power over the tides, and when the sun, moon, and earth are in alignment, in a process called syzygy, the gravitational pull of the three on our tides is phenomenal, and this is when we have high tides known as spring tides.[10]

10. Stroud, *The Book of the Moon.*

A DAY ON THE MOON

The moon has days, believe it or not, and the length of a lunar day is 27.3 earth days. This is known as the Sidereal month, which is the shortest of the moon cycles. The moon has its own cycles, with the main three being the Synodic month, which takes 29.5 days to travel from one new moon to the next; the Sidereal month; and the Metonic cycle. The Metonic cycle is the longest of the three as it takes nineteen years for the moon to reappear in exactly the same part of the sky.[11]

Surface

The surface of the moon has some amazing structures caused by billions of years of asteroids and meteors and all manner of debris colliding with it, causing craters and formations that scientists are continuingly studying. The highest mountains on the moon are over 16,000 feet, while its deepest craters are over 15,000 feet with the widest of

11. Stroud, *The Book of the Moon*.

these craters being over 140 miles in diameter, which is just astounding when you think of it.[12]

The surface of the moon has three main features. The first is the *Terrae* or highlands, which are made up of craters left by objects impacting the moon. Second, the *Maria* or seas, which are the large dark circular objects we can see from earth when we look at the moon. These seas have some of the most beautiful names, such as the Sea of Tranquillity, the Sea of Crises, the Sea of Nectar, the Sea of Cold, and the Sea of the Edge, to name but a few.[13]

The moon is not only home to twenty seas, but fourteen bays, which have names such as the Bay of Rainbows, while the twenty lakes have names such as the Lake of Forgetfulness; the one ocean is named the Ocean of Storms. These are not actual water bodies as the moon has no water on its surface, but ancient astronomers thought the dark

12. Stroud, *The Book of the Moon*.

13. Ezzy Pearson and Iain Todd, "Lunar Maria: A Complete Guide to the Seas of the Moon," *Sky at Night Magazine*, July 28, 2020, https://www.skyatnightmagazine.com/space-science/lunar-maria-guide-list-seas-moon/.

areas on the moon were indeed seas and therefore named them as such.[14]

The third main feature of the moon's surface is the *Regolith*, which is a layer of dust that covers almost all the moon's surface.

Climate

There is no atmosphere on the moon like earth, and there is no air to breathe. However, there is a very thin layer of gases on the lunar surface called an exosphere. The moon is a very inhospitable place with the average temperature during the day tipping to 134 C (273 F) and dropping to -154 C (-245 F) at night.[15]

MOON CYCLES

The moon has eight cycles, and at the very beginning of the cycle, we do not see the moon. It is in complete darkness;

14. Jeffrey Kluger, "Earth's Great Gift to the Moon: Water," *Time*, May 10, 2013, https://science.time.com/2013/05/10/lunar-water/.

15. Tim Sharp, "Atmosphere of the Moon," Space, last updated February 28, 2022, https://www.space.com/18067-moon-atmosphere.html.

it is invisible. The moon then gradually begins to appear to us night after night as it grows from a tiny silver crescent whose horns, or tops, point to the left, which is called the waxing crescent. As the moon continues its cycle, it grows into the first quarter, which we see as the half moon, and then it develops into the waxing gibbous, almost full in appearance. The final part of this growing stage is the full moon, of which there are three nights; it then begins its decrease as it wanes. The first part of this is the waning gibbous, then the last quarter, and finally the waning crescent—this time the horns on the top of the moon are pointing to the right. And then the moon disappears for the cycle to begin again.

Wax On, Wane Off

In each of these cycles, we see the moon in its various stages, to which we attribute various correspondences and meanings. These are the stages or phases known as waxing, waning, gibbous, full moon, and new moon. These terms stem from Old English; for example, *waxing* is derived from

weaxen, which means "to increase." *Waning* stems from *wanian*, which means "to lessen," and *gibbous* is derived from a Latin term meaning "hump," which is *gibbus*.

Many spell weavers will make sure the moon is waxing or waning before they cast a spell. Essentially, if the moon is waxing, you are bringing something to you, and if it is waning, you are sending something away from you. In magical terms, waxing means to invoke, waning means to banish.

It is easier nowadays to determine the phases of the moon as many apps, which can be installed on phones, tell you when the moon is waxing or waning usually in a weather app, but there are specific moon ones.

Moon Void-of-Course

When casting spells and using your magical practices, please be aware of what phase the moon is in as there are a few occasions in which spell weaving is not recommended. One of those times is during an eclipse, and the other is void-of-course, or simply moon void.

As the moon has its cycles, it moves into different planetary signs of the zodiac. The moon void-of-course is the

time just before the moon enters a new sign—a sort of no-man's-land exists where nothingness and emptiness prevail. No magical intentions should take place when the moon is void as spells and any magical activities will turn out very differently, usually negatively, if they come to fruition at all.

Dark Moon

The dark moon is that time between the full moon ending and a new moon emerging. It is the dark nights when no moon is visible to us, but rest assured, she is still there; she's just not showing. These are the nights when dreamwork and psychic development can be exercised, and you can work on your scrying techniques. Scrying is when you look into the future by using various traditional techniques, such as by mirror, water, or flame. One famous scryer was Nostradamus (1503–1566), whose works are still read today. The dark moon is also an ideal time to work on seeing into the dark and to ceremonially bathe to release negative thoughts and energies that have built up throughout the month.

REACHING FOR THE MOON

The race to the moon began as early as 1946 when the United States of America bounced radio waves off the moon, but the real Space Race truly began when the Soviet Union launched Sputnik in 1957. Then, in 1961, President Kennedy handed the baton to NASA with his speech to congress, igniting the rocket of space discovery. He said, "I believe that this nation should commit itself to achieving the goal, before this decade is out, of landing a man on the moon and returning him safely to the earth."[16]

Sadly, President Kennedy would not live to see his words become reality, but in July 1969, Apollo 11 touched down upon the moon, in the geographical location of the Sea of Tranquillity. The world held its breath as Neil Armstrong

16. John F. Kennedy, "Address at Rice University on the Nation's Space Effort," September 12, 1962, transcript, https://www.jfklibrary.org /learn/about-jfk/historic-speeches/address-at-rice-university-on-the -nations-space-effort.

spoke those immortal words: "One small step for man, one giant leap for mankind."[17]

The grainy grey pictures transmitted around the world to television sets in many homes; many people had bought their television sets just for the occasion. Indeed, many people had moon landing parties and watched this historic event with friends and family.

However, even at the time of the moon landings in 1969, the controversy regarding the event had already begun as some people did not believe what they were seeing. My mother was one of them and, to this day, still does not believe we went to the moon. The moon landings are one of the main conspiracies in the world with many people now not believing we ever made it to the moon.[18]

17. The Associated Press, "Armstong's Famous 'One Small Step' Quote—Explained," AP News, July 13, 2019, https://apnews.com /article/neil-armstrong-ap-top-news-fl-state-wire-tx-state-wire -apollo-11-moon-landing-c0d6977d310042af96bb7e2e3287a268.

18. Elizabeth Howell, "Moon-Landing Hoax Still Lives On. But Why?" January 25, 2022, https://www.space.com/apollo-11-moon-landing -hoax-believers.html.

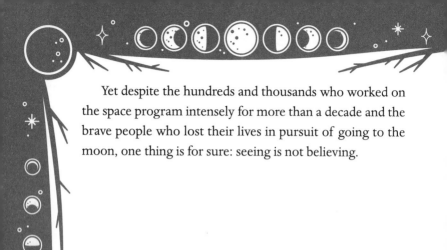

Yet despite the hundreds and thousands who worked on the space program intensely for more than a decade and the brave people who lost their lives in pursuit of going to the moon, one thing is for sure: seeing is not believing.

Getting Started

When working magically and in harmony with the moon, there are a few items I suggest you have on hand before you begin your journey. These tools and supplies can be gathered over time, but chances are you probably have most of these items on hand right now.

Did you know the full moon is a wonderful time to have clearouts and cleanups? Use the full moon to look for your basic tools and supplies. Clear a cupboard, wardrobe, or even a particular room; you never know what you will find. Why is the full moon an ideal time for this work? Its energy is perfect for doing something you have been putting off. The full moon energies can shine light upon areas we have delayed sorting because of the mundane feeling they

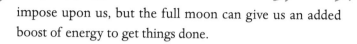

impose upon us, but the full moon can give us an added boost of energy to get things done.

MOON JOURNAL

Purchase or make yourself a journal or notebook to keep all your moon information in. One of the handy things about a moon journal is that you do not need to write in it every day like a diary. You can write in it only on full moons, so once or twice a month (which is quite good if you are anything like me). Diaries need to be written in every day preferably, but this can be time consuming. With a moon journal, you are not under pressure to write in it daily.

Use the moon journal to record phases of the moon, moon spells, moon affirmations and wishes, or things connected to the moon called correspondences. Also, write how you feel during different phases of the moon. For example, do you feel you have an extra amount of energy during the full moon, or are you restless and cannot sleep?

Always keep your moon journal safe, and if you buy a hefty notebook, your journal can last not just twelve months, but years—mine is over five years old.

MOON ALTAR

It is always nice to have a special place in your home or garden to keep all things moon related. Many practitioners of magic will have a specific place in their garden where they will perform rituals all throughout the year. In the northern hemisphere in the depths of winter, it is not always advisable to spend a considerable amount of time outside at night due to the extreme cold temperatures. Instead, a specific place in your home can become your altar, from a shelf or corner to a whole table, depending on your needs.

On your altar, you can place relevant symbols or your moon practice, such as white candles, an image or picture of the moon deity you may wish to work with, and perhaps an offering, such as moon cakes or milk.

MOON CHART

It is handy to have a moon chart that depicts the moon in its various phases throughout the year. A good lunar calendar can also tell you this information. However, many weather apps can tell you this information, too, so check your phone. Also, just watch the moon; you will be able to

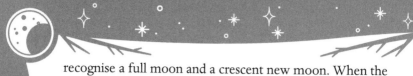

recognise a full moon and a crescent new moon. When the moon is waxing, the tips of the moon's horns are pointing left; when the moon is waning or diminishing, the horns are pointing right.

A moon chart is handy to plan things against, especially if you find yourself having sleepless nights or difficulty concentrating during the full moon.

MOON BOX

As you begin to work with the moon, you may start to grow a rather large selection of resources from oils to crystals. Depending on the size of your moon collection, it is advisable and practical to keep everything together. An old shoebox that you can decorate with moon symbols is ideal if your collection is not too big, and if you have amassed many resources, then a moon cupboard in your kitchen, office, or bedroom will be perfect to keep all your moon items in. Once again, decorate the cupboard if you wish with moon symbols.

MOON CANDLES

Candles are another good resource to have; however, instead of buying all manner of different colours for ritual, just make sure to have white candles of varying shapes and sizes. Tealight candles burn down quickly and do not take up much room, whereas pillar candles can be huge. It all depends on your needs, space, and budget.

The other recommended candle for moon work is a black candle. Generally, a black candle is used during specific lunar occurrences and phases, such as an eclipse or the dark moon. However, be sure to burn the white candle alongside the black as magic is always about balance and the white will counteract any negative influences that may be roaming freely.

IN ESOTERICA

The moon features in several esoteric beliefs, especially in tarot and astrology. It is important to recognize the moon's meaning in these occult systems as no matter our sun sign, we all have a moon sign that can influence our lives if it is the stronger sign of the two.

The Moon in Tarot

The tarot is a set of seventy-eight playing cards used for divinatory purposes. These cards are divided into two sets: the Major Arcana cards number one to twenty-one and are often regarded as the most powerful and spiritual cards of the deck; the following fifty-six cards are known as the Minor Arcana and are divided into suits, which consist of Wands, Swords, Pentacles, and Cups. One of the Major Arcana cards is The Moon, and this card is probably one of the most mysterious and esoteric cards in the entire deck. With its pictorial images of usually a full moon and a stream or some form of running water, this card corresponds to water, emotions, and hidden things.

The Moon card can represent the dark mysteries contained within the questioner and can also signify someone who is suffering from insomnia. The Moon card is the dark night of the soul and can also be a warning for people to seek help with their mental health. The Moon card represents the illusionary and deceptive character of the moon itself and thereby the questioner.

The Moon in Astrology

The moon in the astrological context forms a central part of our birth charts. Just as we have the star or sun sign, which reflects our outward personality, we also have a moon zodiac sign, which dwells on the other side of us and controls our emotions and moods. The moon sign is where our dreams, hopes, and fears reside. For some astrologers, the moon sign is one of the most important areas in your birth chart and may outshine your sun sign. For example, my sun sign is Pisces, a water sign; however, my moon sign is Sagittarius, a fire sign. I am not only fire and water, but in certain areas, the moon sign shines brighter.

The moon is associated with our emotional responses. Its position in our birth charts and which zodiac house it falls in can explain much about our personalities and desires. For example, if the moon is positioned in a water sign (Pisces, Cancer, or Scorpio), this can indicate a highly sensitive and moody individual. In a fire sign (Aries, Leo, and Sagittarius), the moon is likely to have produced an individual who expresses themselves easily and usually with brutal honesty. Those born with their moon in an air sign

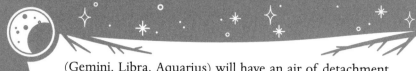

(Gemini, Libra, Aquarius) will have an air of detachment and coolness about them. Finally, those who are born with the moon in the earth signs (Taurus, Virgo, or Capricorn) may find self-expression rather difficult.

There is one zodiac sign that has the moon as its ruling planet, and that is Cancer, the sign of the water crab. These individuals born between June 20 and July 22 are water signs and are renowned for being rather moody due to their ruling planet, the moon. Cancer individuals can be protective, tenacious, tough, caring, and extremely protective of their loved ones. Cancer individuals, due to the moon's influence, are incredibly loving and motherly and enjoy nothing better than making a safe and secure environment, but just like the crab of their symbol, they are incredibly tough and protective of their inner life, loves, and dreams.

Lunar Lore

The moon's presence has seeped into our culture in many ways from superstitions to theatre and films, to our very language. The moon appears on ancient documents and tablets from a time long passed, such as on cave paintings and ancient megaliths.

The Lascaux Cave paintings from the Dordogne Valley in France were created by our hunter-gatherer ancestors in 14,000 BCE.[19] Upon the cave are images of horses and a lunar cycle, which is represented by twenty-nine dots. In Ireland, at one of the world's most sacred prehistoric sites, Newgrange, there is an inscription that appears to depict

19. Visit https://www.bradshawfoundation.com/lascaux/ to learn more.

the lunar cycle of a left crescent, a full moon, and a right crescent. These lunar images were created over five thousand years ago, and yet the lunar inscription on this Neolithic monument resembles the modern code of lunar symbols.[20] We build upon our ancestors' work, and our ancestors adhered to the moon.

THE FARMER'S ALMANAC

One of the main ways the moon has found its way into our culture is by the names we have bestowed upon it, the most common of which can be found in the famous Farmer's Almanac. These names represent the connection the moon has within our environment and the passing year. The full moon of every month was given a name that corresponded with what was happening in the natural world, whether it was harvest time or the snow was on the ground.

The following are the traditional moon names and their meanings found in the almanac.

20. Visit https://www.newgrange.com/ to learn more.

January
Cold Moon

January in the northern hemisphere is often the coldest month of the year, hence the name Cold Moon. However, in places where wolves roam freely, it is also called the Wolf Moon. At this time, hungry wolves scour the woods and forests looking for food. The other more recent name for the January moon is the Old Moon, but this is rarely used now—though all the names are recognised and can be used to describe the first month of the year.

February
Quickening Moon

The February moon is called the Quickening Moon as nature seems to speed up now and everything appears to grow; there is life stirring within the earth. Although still a month of winter, February for many heralds the beginning of spring, with aconites and snowdrops making their appearance from the cold snowy earth of winter. However, the snowy weather is responsible for the other name given to February's full moon: Snow Moon. The other name is

Hungry Moon, as by February winter food stocks are running low and people and animals could go hungry this month.

March

Storm Moon

March is a temperamental month in the northern hemisphere with sudden changes expected in weather. The old farmer's saying of "March comes in like a lion and goes out like a lamb," or vice versa is an indicator of the storms and gales this month brings. Therefore, it is no surprise that the moon of this month is called the Storm Moon. The other names for this month's moon are the Worm Moon and the Sap Moon, as the earth begins to warm and soften, earthworms begin to stir, and tree sap begins to flow.

April

Wind Moon

As March brings the storms with warm spring temperatures meeting the final cold snaps of winter weather, April sees

the jet stream and other weather systems switching and moving subtly, bringing gales and strong winds swirling around the earth. The Wind Moon of April is the indicator of the expected dominant weather of this month. More subtly, the other common name for April's moon is the Pink Moon due to the flowers that are in bloom during this month. The other less common names are Fish Moon, Egg Moon, and even Sprouting Grass Moon—these all explain what is happening in nature during April, from the grass growing to the fish mating and breeding.

May
Flower Moon

The moon of May is one that echoes the bountiful beauty in nature and flowers. The common saying of "April showers bring forth May flowers" shows how one month leads into the next and nature follows suit. May is a time of abundance in nature as all manner of plants and animals are in full bloom and bounty. Other names for May's moon are the Corn Moon and the Milk Moon.

June

Strong Sun Moon

June in the northern hemisphere brings with it the summer solstice, which heralds the turning time of the year as this is the most powerful the sun will be. June's moon is also commonly called Strawberry Moon as the strawberries are ready to be picked. The other name is from the flower in full bloom during this month: Rose Moon.

July

Blessing Moon

The Blessing Moon is so called due to this month's blessings and abundance of nature. With flowers and early fruits such as soft berries being readily available, July was always regarded as a month of blessings from nature, and so the moon was readily named as such. The other names for this month also indicate the abundance of nature: Meadow Moon, Buck Moon, and Thunder Moon. July's moon was called the Buck Moon due to the male deer having regrown their antlers by this time, and "Thunder Moon" was due to

the hot summer thunderstorms that tend to prevail during this month.

August

Corn Moon

August is the traditional month when corn can be harvested, and indeed, we have the first harvest festival of the year: the Blessing of Loaves. Thus, this moon was given the prevailing name of Corn Moon. It is also called the Green Corn Moon and the Red Moon. Another common name is the Sturgeon Moon as this is their breeding period and they were readily caught at this time.

September

Harvest Moon

September is the traditional time of the harvest. Crops, fruits, and vegetables are brought in from the fields as people stock up for the coming winter. The Harvest Full Moon of September is a welcome sight for many farmers as they work long into the night bringing in nature's bounty. The other name for this month's moon is an indicator of

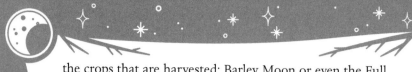

the crops that are harvested: Barley Moon or even the Full Corn Moon. Some people also call this moon the Apple Moon due to the apples being harvested at this time.

October

Blood Moon

"The Blood Moon of October" is probably one of the most famous moon names and has gone down in legends pertaining to all manner of supernatural myths, such as werewolves, witches, and vampires. October is the month of Halloween and the middle of autumn, a season of change within nature that brings mysterious weather phenomena of mists and fog. The reason for the name "Blood Moon" was due in part to October signalling hunting season, which also explains this moon's other name: the Hunter's Moon. This moon can appear red or orange as eclipses are common in October. The lesser-known name for this month's moon is the Sanguine Moon due to the colour the moon becomes during an eclipse.

November

Mourning Moon

There are several reasons why November's moon is called the Mourning Moon. One of the most obvious is because we are in mourning for the summer. November, although the final month of autumn, often heralds the beginning of the long cold winter with shortened days and cold temperatures. November is also the traditional month of Libitina, the ancient Roman goddess of funerals and death, so perhaps this belief has found its way into our consciousness through the centuries. On a more cheerful note, the other names for this month's moon are the Beaver Moon, as this is the time when beavers are busy building dams for the winter, and the Frost Moon, as November is traditionally when the first frosts begin.

December

Long Nights Moon

December is the final month of the year for many and the month in which the winter solstice occurs. The shortest day gives way to the longest night, hence "Long Nights Moon." In the northern hemisphere, this is also traditionally a cold month, and so Cold Moon is another name. Other names include the Moon Before Yule Moon or even the Oak Moon, as the Oak King begins his journey back into full bloom in June, just a short six months away during the longed-for days of summer.

MOON DAY

The moon has also influenced how we calculate time and the days of the week. It is believed that the seven-day week originated with the ancient Babylonians, who divided the lunar month into four lots of seven days.[21] These were named after the planets that are visible to the naked eye. Through the twists and turns of history and language from the Babylonians to the Egyptians, Greeks, and Romans, to Latin and French, we arrive at what we have today in the English language:

---

21. John M. Steele, *The Circulation of Astronomical Knowledge in the Ancient World: Time, Astronomy, and Calendars* (Boston: Brill, 2016).

Monday	Moon	dies Lunae	Lundi
Tuesday	Mars	dies Martis	Mardi
Wednesday	Mercury	dies Mercurii	Mercredi
Thursday	Jupiter	dies Jovis	Jeudi
Friday	Venus	dies Veneris	Vendredi
Saturday	Saturn	dies Saturni	Samedi
Sunday	Sun	dies Solis	Dimanche

Each day of the week has a correspondence that coincides with the planet and the god it is named after; of course, these gods and planets are responsible for several attributes.

Monday

Monday is named for the moon and rules the home, politics, business, memory, psychic ability, intuition, and women's power. The stone associated with Monday is moonstone.

Tuesday

Tuesday coincides with Mars, a male god of war, so it is associated with physical energy, sex, passion, desire, ambition, force, power, work, competition, and (interestingly) healing! Its stone is ruby.

Wednesday

Wednesday is Mercury's Day. Mercury, or his Greek identity Hermes, was the messenger of the gods. He is often depicted with wings on his sandals or feet. So, magical workings on a Wednesday are associated with rapid change, magical ability, speech, writing, knowledge, rational thought, and intellect. The stone is opal.

Thursday

Thursday is for Jupiter, Mr. Big himself, the biggest planet in our solar system. His correspondences are growth, expansion, luck, abundance, career, leisure, time, optimism, prosperity, and aspirations. His stone is amethyst.

Friday

Friday is the day of Venus, goddess of love, so of course Friday rules the arts, beauty, fertility, fruition, grace, love, security, marriage, harmony, and money. Today's stone is emerald.

Saturday

Saturn can be a bit of a dark influence, I've found, but his connections are to karma, past lives, reincarnation, work, and reality. The stone is onyx.

Sunday

We all love the good old sun; therefore, we get joy, happiness, completion, health, men's power, leadership, pleasure, success, and authority with this day. Its stone is gold or goldstone.

MOON SUPERSTITIONS

Another way the moon influences our cultural consciousness is through superstitions. I grew up with many moon

superstitions; one of them my father constantly told me off for. *Do not stare at the moon through glass otherwise bad luck will follow.* However, I continue to stare at the moon whenever I see her—she is hypnotic, after all.

Nevertheless, here are some superstitions regarding the moon you may have heard of.

- A baby born during a full moon is a child of fortune.
- Move house on a new moon.
- Cut hair and nails during a waning moon.
- If you see the new moon over your right shoulder, you will be lucky; if over the left, you will be unlucky; and straight ahead is good fortune.
- Rub warts with dirt while looking at the moon—this will cure them.
- Pointing at the moon brings bad luck; pointing at the first new moon of the year brings twelve months of sorrow.
- Marry during a full moon.

- Count your money on a new moon as it will increase.

- On the night of the new moon, turn your money in your pocket over and think about being lucky.

- Bow three times to the new moon and make a wish.

Myths and Legends

One of my favourite myths about the moon is the Man in the Moon. In many seaside towns across England, there was always an illumination with a crescent moon and a man or character inside it lighting up the promenade. The other wonderful myth about the moon was that it was made of cheese. In 2002, NASA played an April Fools' joke on the world by declaring they had proof the moon was made of cheese after discovering an expiration date printed on the moon, which sadly, of course, was a hoax.

One of the main legends that has seeped into our psyche regarding the moon is that of the werewolf. Indeed, the entire legend surrounding the werewolf corresponds to the phases of the moon and especially the full moon—specifically, the

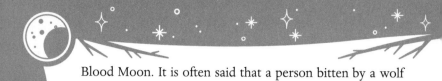

Blood Moon. It is often said that a person bitten by a wolf during the Blood Moon will become a werewolf.

WEREWOLVES

Throughout the world, there are countless stories of werewolves. There are many sayings and customs pertaining to them, such as in Greece, where it is believed that eyebrows meeting above the nose indicates a werewolf. In Britain, we have our own similar belief: "Beware of those whose eyebrows meet, for in their hearts lies deceit," though this really just means they are not to be trusted. Other indicators of a werewolf are clawlike fingers and small pointed ears.

There are many ways in which a person might become a werewolf. One of them is by heredity, in which case there is nothing much you can do about it. Another is that you are bitten by a werewolf, in which case do not eat anyone for nine years and you will be fine! The other way you might become a werewolf is through enchantment by a witch. People believed the witches' spells could be broken if you pointed at the victim in their human form and shouted, "You are the wolf!" three times. Failing that, you could call out their Christian name three times while they were in their wolf form. Failing that, run! However, as with all witches' spells, if you did try to break the spell, there was always the possibility the curse could transfer to you!

A werewolf is nothing more than a shapeshifter. There are countless stories of shapeshifting gods and goddesses, shamans, and medicine men. The possibility of shapeshifting, of transforming yourself into something else, has been explored since the beginning of time. You can take on the attributes of your animal of choice—the strength of a bear, the ferociousness of a lion, the stealth of a snake, the wisdom of an owl, or the independence of a lone wolf. And all these transformations, of course, involve a ritual underneath a full moon.

Animal Strengths Shapeshifting Spell
Moon Phase: Full Moon
Need: Moon journal, pen, paper, picture of an animal

If you wish to use the strengths of an animal for a particular reason, such as the wisdom of an owl for an exam or the agility of a cat for an exercise routine, try this modern

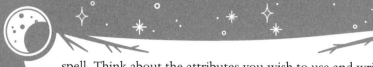

spell. Think about the attributes you wish to use and write them on a piece of paper or in your moon journal. Next to this, write your weaknesses in that area—perhaps there is something you just cannot do no matter how much you try, but that comes very easily to this animal, insect, or fish. Have a picture of your desired animal and place it next to your writing.

On the night of a full moon, if possible, go outside to cast this spell. Try to sit in a moonbeam with the photo and writing in front of you. Place both hands over each and say,

> *I take upon the skills of [whatever animal],*
> *In order to strengthen my [weakness].*
> *From this time until the [work] ends,*
> *Animal strength I will spend.*
> *Full moon power, come to me.*
> *My inner animal becomes free.*

Sit for some time in the moonbeam, feeling how the strength and energy of your chosen animal make you powerful. Keep the photo and words together and continue with your planned activity. When it is all over, give thanks to that particular animal by donating to an animal charity or shelter. However you give thanks, it must be animal related.

GREEN CHEESE

One of the earliest written records regarding the moon and cheese comes from John Heywood's writing in 1546. Heywood wrote a book of proverbs, and many of the sayings we have today are from him, such as "the more the merrier" and "a penny for your thoughts." The interesting thing about the moon being made of "greene cheese" is the spelling, as it is not referring to the colour of the cheese but rather to the age of the cheese and, therefore, to the age of the moon.[22] Yet, this idea of the moon being made of cheese was nothing new, even in Tudor England. The following ancient Slavic tale about a hungry wolf and a sly fox was centuries old when John Heywood wrote his proverb: "The moon is made of greene cheese."

In the tale, the wolf chases the fox all over the forest until they reach a pond. The wolf wants to devour the fox

22. John Heywood, *The Proverbs of John Heywood* (London: Forgotten Books, 2016).

but is overcome with thirst from all the running, and as he leans in to drink from the pond, he sees the moon reflected in the water. The clever fox sees an opportunity to escape from the clutches of the wolf and tells him the moon's reflection is actually a block of cheese. He tells the wolf that if he wants the cheese, he must drink all the water first, and so the wolf drinks all the water in the pond until he bursts, and the fox escapes.[23] The moral of the story is of course brains over brawn, and this story has been told throughout the centuries in various ways. The moon's reflection is always a central component in many of these brains-over-brawn stories, such as in the story of the moonraker.

MOONRAKER

People who are born in the county of Wiltshire in southwest England are often termed *moonrakers* due to the canny and enterprising nature of their past citizens. During the seventeenth and eighteenth centuries, there was a heavy price to pay on excise duty on alcohol, especially gin. To counteract this, the Wiltshire men devised a canny way of

23. John T. Naake, *Slavonic Fairy Tales* (Independently Published, 2018).

smuggling it in. They would hide the barrels of alcohol in village ponds and lakes and retrieve their bounty at night. However, one clear full moon night, things went a little wrong.

As they pulled the barrels up from the pond with their rakes, the excise men came upon the scene. In a flash of inspirational genius, the Wiltshire smugglers began to rake the pond. When asked by the duty officers what they were doing, they pointed to the moon's reflection on the pond—they were trying to rake out a piece of the moon that had fallen from the sky. The excise men scoffed at the Wiltshire locals, the "ignorant simpletons," and rode on, leaving the smugglers to carry on with their night's work.[24] To this day, people born in Wiltshire are still referred to as moonrakers, and I am very proud to call myself one, too, having been born in the county.

---

24. Ellen Castelow, "The Moonrakers and Gin Smugglers of Wiltshire," Historic UK, accessed January 19, 2023, https://www.historic-uk .com/CultureUK/The-Moonrakers/.

THE MAN IN THE MOON

The man in the moon became the main figure in many myths and legends. In some myths, he is said to be a man punished by God for collecting sticks on the sabbath, while others believe he is Cain himself, punished by God and banished to the moon for killing his brother, Abel, whom he was jealous of.[25]

Before the onset of space travel and the Apollo moon landings, people believed there was a man on the moon as they could see a man's face peering down, looking at them. This is the phenomenon known as pareidolia—seeing familiar shapes and faces in inanimate objects, such as in clouds, slices of toast, vegetables, fruits, and other places.

We now know there is no one living on the moon given its inhospitable environment, but perhaps one day we will inhabit it with our technological advancements.

25. Roman Catholic Imperialist, "Cain Is the Man in the Moon," Roman Catholic Imperialist, December 28, 2011, https://www.roman catholicimperialist.com/2011/12/cain-is-man-in-moon.html.

Pareidolia Spell

Moon Phase: Full Moon
Need: Moon journal, pen, paper, white tealight candle

If at times you see things that are not there or if there is a certain situation you are not seeing clearly, perform this spell on a full moon. Write the problem or situation in your moon journal and light a white candle. Stare at the problem you have written and say these words:

> *Am I seeing things that are not there?*
> *Do I trust the moon's glare?*
> *Am I wrong or am I right?*
> *What is before my sight?*
> *Show me what my eyes really see.*
> *Show me all that lies before me.*

Cover your eyes with both hands and use your third eye. The third eye is between your eyebrows and slightly higher; it is where your psychic abilities lie, and these need to be exercised regularly. Visualise everything happening around the situation or image, and then remove your hands and

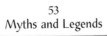

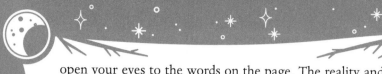

open your eyes to the words on the page. The reality and truth will lie before you or emerge by the new moon.

THE MOON RABBIT/HARE

Another excellent example of pareidolia is the moon rabbit or hare. The dark markings on the moon are said to form the shape of a rabbit or hare—somehow, I just do not see it. However, many people have seen the moon hare, and it forms many stories in Asian countries such as China, Japan, and Korea. In Chinese myth, he can be seen pounding the elixir of life for the moon goddess Chang'e. In Japan and Korea, he is making rice cakes. Interestingly, the moon hare or rabbit features in Mayan and Aztec myths and can be found in South American art, hieroglyphs, and inscriptions. His myth carried far and wide; to see him, just look up at the moon.

Deities and Beings

Throughout time, our ancient people have marvelled at the moon, and as it moved through its lunar cycles, they assigned it divine powers. In the patriarchal religions of Judaism, Christianity, and Islam, the moon and its glory and connections to ancient deities are hidden in plain sight. There are several references throughout the bible to ancient cultures that worshipped the moon. For example, the city of Jericho was named after a moon god. The name *Jericho* literally translates to "City of Moon" and is a gender-neutral name.[26]

---

26. Abarim Publications, "The Amazing Name Jericho: Meaning and Etymology," Abarim Publications, last updated May 13, 2022, https://www.abarim-publications.com/Meaning/Jericho.html.

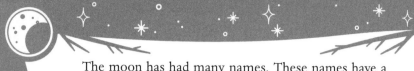

The moon has had many names. These names have a plethora of legends attached to them and are as beautiful as they are varied. These stories try to explain the moon's rhythm throughout its monthly cycle. The moon's disappearance or fullness for three nights was explained through stories of hope, fear, dismay, bravery, monsters, and ghosts.

THE MOON AS FEMALE

Most deities attached to moon worship are female with a few exceptions, such as the popular ancient Egyptian god Thoth, who is the god of wisdom, weigher of hearts, and scribe of gods. One reason the moon is regarded as female is that ancient people associated the divine feminine with the menstrual cycles of women, which correlate with the phases of the moon.

The stages of a woman's life (Maiden, Mother, and Crone) are represented by the phases of the moon, too, and are connected to the Goddess. Here are some modern examples of how we can honour the divine feminine goddesses through all the cycles of the moon.

Aradia

Pantheon: Roman
Name: Goddess of Witches
Moon Phase: New Moon
Colour: Silver
Identification: Maiden

Aradia is an interesting goddess as there are many stories concerning her origins and who she really was. Some believe she was the moon goddess Diana's daughter sent to earth by her mother to teach humans witchcraft. She has, therefore, become a central figure in Wiccan and Neopagan practices and is often called Goddess of Witches. Her story is featured in the 1899 book by Charles Godfrey Leland, *Aradia, or the Gospel of Witches*, in which he discusses her creation story and subsequent practices. The Italian goddess of the witches is credited with creating witches and being the first witch of the world. Aradia was able to teach her practices and secrets to others who became the first coven.

There are many practices that have developed because of the worship of Aradia, with rituals, ceremonies, invocations, and incantations addressed to her. Practitioners also

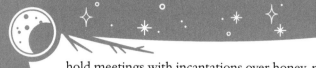

hold meetings with incantations over honey, meal, salt, and wine cakes at a witches' supper, very similar to what was practiced in classical Rome.

The herbs sacred to Aradia are vervain and rue; the cakes are made of rye meal, wine, salt, and honey and formed into a crescent moon. Wholemeal rye flour, widely used in Roman times, makes dark rye bread, which you can try your hand at making if you feel a connection to Aradia.

Aradia Crescent Moon Cake

1 cup (120 grams) wholemeal rye flour
½ cup (60 grams) honey
3 tablespoons red wine
1 teaspoon salt

Preheat the oven to 350°F (180°C). Mix all the ingredients together and shape the dough into a crescent moon. You can either line a baking tray or wrap your crescent moon cake with greaseproof paper to cook so the cake keeps its shape. Put the cake in the oven for thirty minutes and check after twenty minutes. It will naturally be dark in colour, so

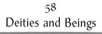

do not assume it has been cooked through; check it with a skewer. If the skewer comes out clean when stuck into the thickest part of the cake, the cake is cooked. Take it out of the oven and leave to cool.

You can use this cake as part of your invitation to Aradia. Light a silver candle, pour a glass of red wine or grape juice, and put some sea salt and honey as well as the cake on your altar. Invite Aradia into your practice and ask her to accept you.

Drink some wine or grape juice, break off a piece of the moon cake, and eat. Sit for some time and watch the candle flame. If it flickers or goes out, Aradia has acknowledged you. Give thanks to the goddess for choosing you to work with and safely extinguish the candle. Leave the offerings of the wine and cake on the altar for a whole day before removing and safely disposing.

Artemis
Pantheon: Greek
Name: Goddess of the Crescent Moon
Moon Phase: Crescent Moon

Colour: Gold
Identification: Maiden

Artemis is the goddess of the hunt and is associated with the crescent moon. She is the goddess of forests and the wilderness and is said to be the Greek equivalent to the goddess Diana, but I think there is something unique about working with this new crescent moon goddess as she brings so much vitality and strength to every pursuit of the month. Ask Artemis to help if you have a challenging month ahead, especially if you are going after something like a promotion, and utilise the power of the new moon.

Artemis Glory of the Hunt Crescent Moon Spell

Moon Phase: New Crescent Moon
Need: Moon journal, pen, paper, fennel seeds

If you have something you are seeking in a certain month, cast this spell on the night of a crescent moon. Write in your moon journal what you want and what you are doing to bring it toward you, such as rewriting your résumé, actively pursuing and applying for jobs, or seeking promotion. Sprinkle some fennel seeds on the page as you say,

> *Goddess of the Crescent Moon,*
> *Who heralds the power of the month,*
> *Give me the strength of the hunt,*
> *The stamina to win the prize.*
> *Glory of the month in my sights.*

Write out the desired result in your moon journal. Write it as a diary entry for the end of that month. For example:

> *March 31*
> *Dear Diary,*
>
> *Today I began my new job and I really enjoyed it.*

Close your journal and keep it on your altar or in a safe place until the spell has come to fruition.

Cerridwen

Pantheon: Welsh
Name: Goddess of the Harvest Moon
Moon Phase: Full Moon
Colour: Yellow
Identification: Crone

The Celtic goddess of rebirth, transformation, and inspiration, Cerridwen is a Welsh goddess who features in many myths and legends, including those of King Arthur. She is known for having many symbols, one of which is the Cauldron of Knowledge; in some legends, this was interpreted to mean the Holy Grail. One of her great potions took a year and a day to reach its potency and was held to grant knowledge and inspiration.

There are many great works of art associated with Cerridwen due to her being the goddess of interpretation, and one of her main artistic pursuits is poetry.

The herb she is associated with most is sage as she is often viewed as the ancient keeper of knowledge and wisdom. She is regarded as the Crone in many witch circles.

Cerridwen Harvest Moon Inspiration Potion
Moon Phase: Full Moon
Need: Sage leaves, water, pan with lid, honey,
    glass jar or bottle

If you are having difficulty in a creative project or you would like to be more creative, brew up some Cerridwen inspiration potion. Gather a handful of fresh sage leaves if you are growing them; if not, get one tablespoon of dried sage leaves. Combine in a pan with two pints of water and bring to a boil. Remove from heat and place a lid on the pan. Allow to steep for at least an hour. After, strain the mixture, removing all the sage leaves, and reheat, adding a half cup of honey. Simmer. Allow the honey to melt. When it has completely dissolved, remove from heat and allow to cool before pouring into a glass jar or bottle.

On the night of the Harvest Moon, leave the potion in the moon's light and ask Cerridwen to bless it. Hold the bottle or jar in your hands and say,

> *Cerridwen of ancient past,*
> *Hear me as I humbly ask,*
> *For you to bless this potion,*
> *With all the power of creativity,*
> *As inspiration now flows to me.*

Leave overnight in view of the moon, and in the morning, label and date your bottle. When you are about to

begin a creative project or need inspiration, drink an egg-cup's worth of the potion.

Diana

Pantheon: Roman
Name: Goddess of the Hunt
Moon Phase: Full Moon
Colour: White
Identification: Mother

The Roman goddess of hunting and the moon, Diana was also known as Artemis in ancient Greece. She is the patron of motherhood and the protector of women during childbirth. Diana is often prayed to and revered by practitioners of magic, regarded by those who worship her as the first goddess of magic, created before all creation.

Diana, like her daughter Aradia, taught magic and sorcery. Diana became known as the Queen of Witches after she showed the fairies, goblins, and other magical folk that she could darken the heavens and turn all the stars into mice. She herself could shapeshift into a cat.

Diana's herbs are rosemary and lavender, and she can bestow many wishes to you.

Diana Full Moon Witches' Stone Gift Charm
Moon Phase: Full Moon
Need: Stone or shell with a hole in it, white tealight candle, ribbon or thin leather cord

To find a stone or shell with a hole in it, often called a witch stone or hagstone, is a special sign of favour from Diana. If you find one, give thanks to Diana on the night of a full moon. Place your witch stone or shell on your altar and light a white candle. Say,

> *Blessed be, great Diana,*
> *Queen of Heaven and of Earth,*
> *Protectress of all.*
> *Thank you for your gift,*
> *For the great gift of magic is sought.*
> *With this stone, good deeds are taught.*
> *Blessed be, great Diana.*

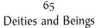

Leave the stone in the moonlight overnight. In the morning, use the stone for any magical practices. Wear or carry your charm wherever you go by keeping it in your purse or car. If your stone or shell is small enough, attach it to some ribbon or thin leather and make a necklace or bracelet of it and wear it for protection.

Hecate

Pantheon: Greek
Name: Goddess of Magic
Moon Phase: Dark Moon
Colour: Black
Identification: Crone

Hecate is a no-messing-around goddess, and she is to be revered probably more than the others—such is her prowess. Although a goddess, she is also part of the Triple Goddess of Greece. She is the goddess of the underworld and is associated with crossroads. Hecate, or Hekate, is probably the most mysterious and feared of the goddesses of magic, being fearless herself—she was the one who, on hearing that Hades had whisked Persephone away to his home in the underworld, grabbed her flaming twin torches and went to get Persephone back, which she did. Unfortunately, as Persephone had already eaten the seeds of death, she had to spend half the year in the underworld. After this time, Persephone could spend the rest of the year with her mother, Demeter.

Hecate, goddess of illumination, accompanies Persephone for the months when she is in the underworld. We know this time as winter. As Hecate spends half the year in the underworld, she is both light and dark. She is often depicted with her three-headed dog, the heads representing past, present, and future. A black dog is her symbol, as are snakes, keys, torches, and a white dress. If you dream of or see a black dog in spirit form, it could mean Hecate is trying to connect with you.

Hecate's throne is in spirit, for she is the essence that moves through all. She is the summer and winter; she is the light and the dark. She is loyal to her followers and extremely foreboding to her enemies, a force of love and a force to be reckoned with. Although her colour is black, through the prism, black light reveals all the colours.

Hecate Quartz Dark Moon Spell

Moon Phase: Any of the three nights the moon is invisible to us

Need: One white and one black tealight candle, clear quartz

If you wish to work with Hecate, be respectful and honour her by always having a white and a black candle on your altar. If you can, get a clear quartz crystal and dedicate it to Hecate. Clean the quartz either by soaking it in salt water for an hour or by wafting an incense stick over it.

Light the candles and say these words:

> *Goddess of dark, goddess of light,*
> *Blessed Hecate, make it right.*
> *This quartz I give to you.*
> *Imbue it with your love and grace.*
> *Help me make the great work of magic.*
> *In your honour, I shall work.*
> *Mighty Hecate, blessed be.*
> *Great Hecate, thank you for choosing me.*
> *An' it harm none, so mote it be.*

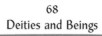

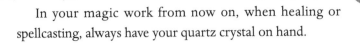

In your magic work from now on, when healing or spellcasting, always have your quartz crystal on hand.

Ishtar

Pantheon: Sumerian
Name: Goddess of Fertility
Moon Phase: Waxing
Colour: Red
Identification: Mother

Ishtar is a rather formidable goddess of sex, war, and love, and she is often regarded as the Queen of the Universe. She is the one we pray to when we are confronted with struggles. To have Ishtar fight on your side is a great honour. Although at times she can be vindictive, she is a fearsome and strong goddess and a great ally to have. She is also known as the goddess of the circle of life as she is associated with both birth and death.

Ishtar is also referred to as the Queen of the Night and can shapeshift, appearing in many forms. Her sacred plants are mugwort, yew, and willow. She is everywhere and

nowhere, for the shapeshifter constantly reinvents herself and can adapt to any environment.

Glamour is a term in magic to describe a practice similar to shapeshifting. Originally, a glamour was regarded as a spell cast by a witch to make somebody see things in a different way, but it later came to refer to a spell that actually changes a person's appearance. If you have a battle coming up—a job interview or any challenging meeting—and need to glamour and portray yourself as strong and confident, the best and the victorious, cast this spell.

Ishtar Waxing Moon Glamour Spell

Moon Phase: Waxing Moon
Need: Photo, red tealight candle, mirror

Place a picture of someone you admire for their strength and courage in front of a mirror. Light a red candle on a waxing moon and say these words:

> *Mother Ishtar, I call upon you.*
> *Change me so that only I can see,*
> *The nature hidden within me.*
> *Let my appearance be strong and true.*

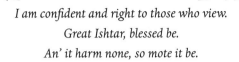

I am confident and right to those who view.
Great Ishtar, blessed be.
An' it harm none, so mote it be.

Look into the picture and the mirror and think about the attributes your role model has. Visualise yourself having the same qualities. Feel yourself becoming strong and confident and keep staring into the mirror until you are happy with what you see. After, safely extinguish the candle and cover the mirror with the photo until your spell has come to fruition, then dispose of the photo, giving thanks.

Isis

Pantheon: Egyptian
Name: Goddess of Healing
Moon Phase: Gibbous
Colour: Blue
Identification: Mother

Although an ancient Egyptian goddess, Isis was and is worshipped throughout the world. She is regarded as the ultimate female power and is not only the moon but also the waters and seas, which she has control over. She is the ulti-

mate healer; after her husband Osiris was killed and cut into fourteen pieces by his brother Set, the parts were distributed all over the world. Isis found all but one piece and brought Osiris back to life with a spell and her healing powers.

Isis and her followers can still be found all over the world. She has an enduring appeal to many practitioners of magic.

Isis Gibbous Moon Healing Spell

Moon Phase: Gibbous Moon

Need: Milk, blue food colouring or butterfly pea flower extract

If you are experiencing low energy, ask Isis, goddess of healing, to build you back up. On a gibbous moon, pour a glass of milk (any milk will suffice; I use soya). Add three drops of blue food dye or the flower extract to the milk (blue is the colour of healing). As you stir, say,

> *Building and growing day by day,*
> *Strength and healing come my way.*

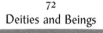

I am happy and I am full of vitality.
Mother Isis, heal me please.

Look at the blue milk, imagine it is the healing blue waters of Isis, and drink. Feel the coolness as it goes down into your body, filling you with strength and vitality.

Juno

Pantheon: Roman
Name: Mother of the Gods
Moon Phase: Full Moon
Colour: Green
Identification: Mother

Juno was deemed the mother of the gods in the ancient Roman pantheon and is often thought of as a female guardian angel—as every man had his genius, so every woman had her Juno.[27] Juno is the matron goddess of motherhood, matrimony, and money. There are many temples across the ancient world where worshippers called upon her help in

27. The Editors of Encyclopaedia Britannica, "Juno: Roman Goddess," Britannica, last updated January 13, 2023, https://www.britannica.com/topic/Juno-Roman-goddess.

these areas during the various phases of the moon. Use the power of the full moon and the mother goddess to ask for help in money matters.

Juno Full Moon Money Spell

Moon Phase: Full Moon
Need: Moon journal, pen, paper, tea

On the first night of the full moon, write the amount of money you want in your moon journal. Then make yourself a cup of tea, and as you stir the tea clockwise, say these words:

> *By the power of the full moon, Juno, I speak of thee.*
> *Hear me, goddess, and know my plea.*
> *By next month's end,*
> *This money amount please send.*

Trace the amount you have written with your right index finger. Then slowly sip the tea, and as you do, underneath the written amount, write what you will spend the money on. Try to break down the figures so Juno can see

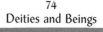

you intend to use the money wisely, for she is a wise and shrewd goddess and will not suffer fools easily.

Luna

Pantheon: Greek
Name: Goddess of the Moon
Moon Phase: Waning
Colour: Indigo
Identification: Maiden, Mother, Crone

Luna is the embodiment of the feminine divine, and as her name implies, she is directly associated with the moon. She is the moon itself, and her power directly corresponds to the mystical and spiritual energy of the moon. Her name literally means "moon" and stems from the Latin *luna*, from which we get so many words: *lunacy*, *lunar*, and so on.

Luna's power is said to ease childbirth and inspire love and lovers. In her ethereal and spiritual aspects, she can mask reality and create illusions. She has the power to manifest all manner of things and is capable of easing and lessening the effects of negative behaviours (which some would argue she caused).

Luna Hex-Breaking Waning Moon Spell

Moon Phase: Waning Moon
Need: String, salt, black tealight candle, photo

If you are feeling off in some way, or things are not going right and everything just feels wrong, you may have been hexed by someone who is jealous of you or just doesn't like you. Indeed, you may feel like someone has put a curse on you. Use the power of Luna on her waning moon to have it taken away.

On the night of a waning moon, place a piece of string in some salt (moon salt is great if you've made some—see page 108). Light a black candle, and if you know the name of the person, write their name down or have a photo of them. If you do not know who put the hex on you, just write *hex* on the paper. Open your arms so your palms are facing upward and make a rising movement with both hands on either side of the candle, as if you were wafting the candlelight toward you. Then say,

> *Luna, goddess of the waning moon,*
> *Break this hex off me and take it away.*

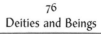

Release this spell from me I say.
No more the bad luck,
This negative feeling of stuck in a rut.
Nothing moves, near or far.
Not matter what I try, no matter how hard.
I beseech, remove this hex from me,
And send it back from whence it came.
I send it back to their name.
I ask ancient rite of three times three.
Luna, please, so mote it be.

Then, taking the string that has been in the salt, wrap the photo and name at least three times. Next, sprinkle the salt on the string-wrapped paper before cutting it in half with a pair of scissors. When the wrapped paper is in two, sprinkle some more salt on the two halves and say, "Begone, begone, begone."

After, sit quietly and watch the flame flicker or completely blow itself out. Imagine the hex physically lifting from you before burying the papers and photo in the garden or carefully burning them.

Selene

Pantheon: Greek
Name: Ultimate Power of the Moon
Moon Phase: All, including the Black Moon
Colour: Black/White
Identification: All, but often depicted as the Maiden

Selene is regarded as the personification of the moon itself. She is particularly influential when it comes to love, and she is said to involve herself in the daily lives of mortals.

She is the source of light for humanity and watches over all, even when we cannot see her. She represents life's constant changes but is steadfast in her strength and love for us. In ancient Greece, special round moon cakes were made and offered during rituals to her.

Invitation to Selene Spell

Moon Phase: Full Moon
Need: Moon journal, pen, paper

You can do this invitation spell at any time during the various nights of the full moon, including those nights when

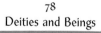

she is not visible. This spell is best performed outdoors in a garden, but any room with moon rays or your moon altar will work. Say these words in front of your altar:

> *Goddess Selene, hear my plea.*
> *I would like to follow thee,*
> *And invite you to work with me.*
> *I see you not in day,*
> *But know that you light my way.*
> *I would like to work with you.*
> *I want to be part of your crew.*

Sit for some time in front of your moon altar and meditate on working with the moon. Keep your moon journal with you, and write down any flashes of inspiration or insight you suddenly have, as these may be coming straight from Selene herself.

THE MOON AS MALE

Male moon gods were strong, protective, and wise, whereas the female moon goddesses were nurturing, motherlike, beautiful, and at times very seductive and dark. Here are just a few prevalent male gods who were given the power of the moon within their cultural setting.

Máni

Pantheon: Norse
Name: Personification of the Moon
Moon Phase: All
Colour: Black/White
Identification: Man in the Moon

In Norse mythology, which shares its beliefs with the northern Germanic tribes, Máni is the personification of the moon and is also the brother of the sun goddess Sol. Unfortunately, at Ragnarök, which is a series of events and catastrophes that signify the end of the world, Máni is destined to be destroyed.

Máni Power-Up Spell
Moon Phase: All
Need: Fennel seeds, lavender, anise, pestle and mortar, small glass jar or bottle

If there is a particular area of your life that requires some *va-va-voom* or you just generally feel stagnant, create this power-up ignition spell to set you back on track.

Crush fennel seeds, lavender, and anise together in a pestle and mortar until small—resembling rice, almost. Place in a little jar or bottle and shake. As you do, say this spell:

> *Power up this little mix.*
> *My life is a mess and needs a fix.*
> *Bless this potion with Black Moon power,*
> *Giving me a zest in every hour.*

Leave the mix below the night sky. In the morning, label and date the bottle, and whenever you need a little extra power in any area of your life, sprinkle a bit of the potion around you. Alternatively, you can put three pinches in a spray bottle of water, shake it up, and spray your office, home, or place of work for extra power.

Odin

Pantheon: Norse
Name: Ultimate Power of the Moon

Moon Phase: All
Colour: Grey / White
Identification: Riding an eight-legged horse

One of my favourite tales of the Norse gods concerning the moon is that of Odin, his eight-footed steed Sleipnir, and the great hunt. On wild November nights when the Hunter's Moon shines upon the land, a great thundering of hooves can be heard across the moonlit sky. This is Odin riding in the Wild Hunt as he gathers souls for Valhalla, the warriors' resting place. The Wild Hunt could also gather souls as people slept. So, if you happen to be out one moonlit night in November and you hear the thundering of hooves, cover your eyes and let the riders pass you by, for if you look upon them, you will be gathered up in the hunt.

Odin's Hunter's Moon Desire Spell

Moon Phase: Full Moon
Need: Moon journal, pen, paper

On the second night of the full moon, write down in your moon journal or on a piece of paper ten attributes and tal-

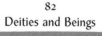

ents you would like your ideal lover to have. Then light a pink candle and say,

I seek you now and ask on this full moon,
If you please, and if you wish, come to me.
My arms are open with love for thee.
I embrace all the new love possibility.

Sit for a while and imagine your ideal person with those talents coming into your life. Imagine what they may look like and how you might meet them. Then extinguish the candle safely. For the next seven days, make sure to do things differently. Take a different bus route home, go to different shops, go to different coffee shops. You are showing the universe you are going out of your way to meet that special someone, and the moon will see this and make sure you will meet.

Nu

Pantheon: Egyptian
Name: Ultimate Power of the Moon
Moon Phase: All

Colour: Gold
Identification: Creation/Exploding Star/Chaos

In the beginning, the male god Nu or Nun is the ultimate creator god of the cosmos, including the moon. Nu is the father of Ra, who is the sun and subsequently becomes the father or grandfather to all the commonly known gods, such as Seth, Horus, Isis, and others.[28] Nu is the oldest of deities and is the beginning of this ancient Egyptian divine family of deities and beings.

Nu Power Storm Spell
Moon Phase: Full Moon
Need: Moon journal, pen, paper

There is indeed something very magical about a good storm—although when it cuts out the power and you are left in the dark, it can be pretty terrifying. However, a good storm at night with flashes of the moon is the perfect

28. The Editors of Encyclopaedia Britannica, "Nun: Egyptian God," Britannica, last modified May 18, 2020, https://www.britannica.com/topic/Nun-Egyptian-god.

opportunity to connect with the god Nu, who created the earth out of chaos.

Use the power of the moon to always shine the light in your home so you can see in more ways than one. During the storm, and preferably on a full moon, light one red candle and, listening to the winds, raise your hands to the sky and say,

Lord Nu, I ask of you,
May no storm clouds block the view.
Let your light shine forth forevermore.
In darkness, may I always find the door.
Father Nu of creation might, please always shine your light,
So I can always find the way thus right.

Watch the candle for a while, staring into the flame, and visualise yourself always in moonlight during the autumn nights. See the light around you, beaming like a lighthouse.

Thoth
Pantheon: Egyptian
Name: God of Wisdom

Moon Phase: All
Colour: Blue / Gold
Identification: Scribe

Thoth is often depicted as an ibis or even as a baboon. He performs many duties, including helping souls cross over—he is responsible for judging the dead, along with Anubis. He is also the god of writing, science, and maths.[29] In many images on ancient tombs and tablets, Thoth wears a crown on which the crescent moon is surmounted by a moon disc. He can be rather formidable as a moon god; if he is angered, he is known to decapitate his adversaries and tear out their hearts.

Thoth Education Spell

Moon Phase: Full Moon
Need: Moon journal, pen, paper

Cast this spell on the night of the full moon. In your moon journal, write the date, and then light a white candle. Focus

---

29. Rosicrucian Egyptian Museum, "Deities in Ancient Egypt—Thoth," Rosicrucian Egyptian Museum, accessed January 25, 2023, https:// egyptianmuseum.org/deities-thoth.

your thoughts on the flame and take a few deep breaths. Think about what you really want to accomplish this year. Is it a new fitness regime and ultimately a new, leaner, and healthier you? Or do you want to affirm academic success in all your grades? Write your affirmation. For example:

I have the power to create the reality I want.
I am manifesting all that aligns
with a healthier version of myself.
I embrace all the fitness, strength, diet,
and healthy lifestyle choices that come my way.
I am manifesting the best grades I have ever gotten this year.
I cast my affirmation to the universe;
hear this spell, and make it well.

As you write these affirmations in your journal, say them out loud and write them in a circle that grows and grows and grows on the page. Each time you write your affirmation, say it out loud until your entire page is full. Look at what you have written, and meditate on how you will accomplish your goals. Then safely extinguish the candle.

ANGELS OF THE MOON

The patriarchal religions of Christianity, Judaism, and Islam all believe in angels, the majority of whom are male and are often referred to as the Sons of God. These divine beings have dominion over the earth, sky, and heavens and are mediators between God and humans. They are also responsible for times, days, months, and planets, including the moon.[30] According to the Book of Enoch, there are seven angels who govern the moon.[31] These seven angels are responsible for many things, but their dominion is the celestial realms of the moon.

Anael

Anael, also known as Haniel, is often regarded as one of the seven archangels. His name means "grace, charm, and favour."[32] In the Museo Soumaya in Mexico City, there is a

---

30. Gustav Davidson, *A Dictionary of Angels* (New York: The Free Press, 1994).

31. R. H. Charles, trans., *The Book of Enoch* (Crane, MO: Defender Publishing, 2016).

32. Davidson, *A Dictionary of Angels*.

fabulous piece of artwork depicting Anael as the regent of the moon.

Gabriel

One of the main archangels who is referred to in all the patriarchal religions and appears in sacred and holy texts of Judaism, Islam, and Christianity. He is the guardian of the moon and Monday. His name is translated as "the strength of God" and he is considered by many to be the lead angel in many areas, second only to Michael, who is the "right hand of God."[33]

Phul

Phul is a guardian of the moon and has many abilities, one of which is his ability to change anything into silver, which is the metal of the moon. Phul is often referred to as one of the Olympian Spirits—seven angelic beings who make their appearance in Renaissance literature, such as *The Secret*

---

33. Charles, *The Book of Enoch*.

Grimoire of Turiel. One of Phul's main powers is extending human life to three hundred years.[34]

Suriel

Suriel, Sariel, or Saraqael is an archangel most notably within Hebrew and Aramaic texts. In the Book of Enoch, he is said to have taught humans about the moon and the lunar cycles.[35]

Tsaphiel

In angel lore or angelology, many angels have interchangeable names and can be mistaken for another angel. Tsaphiel can often be regarded as Zaphkiel and Jophiel, but these are all entirely different angels.[36] Tsaphiel protects the moon from other celestial threats, such as comets and meteors.

34. Arthur Edward Waite, *The Book of Ceremonial Magic* (Eastford, CT: Martino Fine Books, 2011).

35. Charles, *The Book of Enoch.*

36. Davidson, *A Dictionary of Angels.*

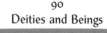

Yahriel

Yahriel is another angel whose name can be written in many ways, including Zachariel and Yehra. Yahriel has the task of governing the moon and is responsible for the moon turning or the smooth running of the lunar cycles.[37]

Zachariel

Zachariel is a very busy angel who not only has dominion of the moon, but also leads souls to judgement. Although this might be frightening to some, he is a friend to humanity and watches over us in every moment.[38]

37. Charles, *The Book of Enoch*.
38. Davidson, *A Dictionary of Angels*.

Moon Energy

The moon influences countless areas of our lives. The moon's power is second only to the sun's, and without both, we simply would cease to be. The moon resonates on such things as salt, water, flowers, and herbs. It can also affect our cooking, sleeping, and appetites, so it is important to look after ourselves during certain moon phases.

I've shown how the moon's celestial rhythm has influenced our belief systems and culture. Now we will explore how the moon associates with magic. All the moon's cycles can be and is utilised for magic. The moon's energy can be harnessed to create resources such as moon salt or moon water, among many others. Furthermore, specific practices

93

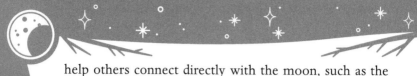

help others connect directly with the moon, such as the Drawing Down the Moon technique.

The moon in magic spreads its light upon every area we can think of, from lunar occurrences of eclipses and equinoxes to the specific practice of Esbat, or honouring the full moon. Moon magic has influenced tarot, crystals, herbs, and all manner of other practices, such as astrology and the power our moon sign has over each and every one of us.

Here, we begin our journey as the moon sheds her light on the magical practices of humans and how Our Lady corresponds with nature.

DRAWING DOWN THE MOON

Drawing Down the Moon was a practice first brought to modern light by the high priestess Doreen Valiente of the Gardnerian tradition of witchcraft. Yet the practice is far older than Wicca of the twentieth century. On an ancient Greek vase, there is a depiction of two women honouring the moon with raised arms; this relic of a past age dates to the second century.[39]

Throughout history, ancient witches and astronomers believed they could command the moon.[40] This practice of connecting with the moon has followed those along the journey of time and finds its way into everyday magical experiences. Witchcraft and the moon have journeyed together, and many honour and revere the moon exactly the way their ancestors did thousands of years ago.

Drawing Down the Moon Spell

Moon Phase: Full Moon
Need: Just you and the moon

On the night of the full moon, go outside and raise your hands above your head to the moon in a Y shape. Allow the moon's rays to flow through the Y of your arms into your

---

39. Margot Adler, *Drawing Down the Moon: Witches, Druids, Goddess-Worshippers, and Other Pagans in America Today* (New York: Viking Press, 1979).

40. Daniel Ogden, *Magic, Witchcraft, and Ghosts in the Greek and Roman Worlds* (New York: Oxford University Press, 2009).

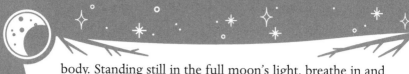

body. Standing still in the full moon's light, breathe in and out and focus your mind and heart, allowing your energy to be infused with the moonlight. When you are ready, say,

> *Lady, I call to you.*
> *Embrace with your light.*
> *Grant my requests this night.*

Stand a little while longer, bathing in the moonlight. When we perform this ritual, we are drawing the moon to us, beckoning her to grace us with magic and energy. Many night rituals and celebrations of the night and the moon herself begin with this practice, as do many spells that call for her power.

ESBATS

The Esbats are one of the times during which Drawing Down the Moon will be performed, more often at the beginning of the ceremony. The Esbat is a full moon ritual celebrated by practitioners of witchcraft and usually involves a coven (a group that practices any form of witchcraft). Many use the Esbat to come together, cast spells, and heal. However, many solitary practitioners use the full moon's power to perform rituals on their own, which involve healing requests for not only friends and family but also for the earth.

Esbat Ritual for Healing the Animal Kingdom

Moon Phase: Full Moon

Need: Moon water spray (see page 104)

If you would like to perform an Esbat on your own or in a group, this is an example ritual to ask the moon to heal the animal kingdom. On any of the nights of a full moon, go outside and, with a spray bottle of moon water and salt (see page 108), spritz in a circle. Make it large enough so you can stand and sit in it. Go around deosil; when you close the circle, you will go widdershins. Raise your hands to the moon, forming the Y shape, and say,

> *Lady of the Moon, wise Goddess of seas and skies,*
> *Look down upon us from on high.*
> *I ask for healing of our brothers and sisters.*

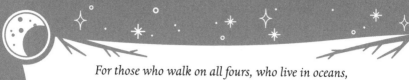

For those who walk on all fours, who live in oceans,
who fly in the air.
For those who live in deserts and mountains,
who crawl upon the earth.
Give us the patience and knowledge to heal our animals,
our friends, and pets.

Kneel and touch the ground with both palms flat on the earth. Say,

I ask for healing of our animal kingdom, here on this earth.
Let us learn from past mistakes
and acknowledge our responsibility from birth.
Goddess of the Moon, I beseech, grant me this request.
I praise you, on high, for now until my final day of rest.

Sit for some time, cross-legged if you can, with your palms flat on the earth beside you, and visualise the power of the moon's rays penetrating the earth, sending healing throughout the land, seas, and sky. When you feel as though you have finished, bow to the moon, say thank you, and go widdershins around your circle, spraying the moon water, saying, "I close this circle; this circle is now closed."

ECLIPSE ENERGY

Eclipses are ideal times to recharge our batteries and take stock of where we are in our lives. Although, it is often advised not to partake in any physical magic such as casting spells during the hours of an eclipse as it is likely to backfire on the caster.

The energy within an eclipse is solely for rest and recuperation and recharging. This has to do with ancient beliefs regarding eclipses, which were often feared because evil was thought to live in the dark. Today, there are still people all around the world who will not even venture out their doors when an eclipse is happening.

Eclipse simply means when one object in space passes through the shadow of another object. There are several types of eclipses. Planets can eclipse each other. On earth, we mostly focus on two specific eclipses: lunar and solar. During these eclipses, these two entities seem to play cat and mouse with the earth.

In magic, a lunar eclipse will emphasise the emotional aspect of human life, whereas a solar eclipse will have a physical emphasis and can affect societies or the financial

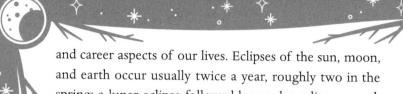

and career aspects of our lives. Eclipses of the sun, moon, and earth occur usually twice a year, roughly two in the spring: a lunar eclipse followed by a solar eclipse a week or so later. The chase between moon and sun occurs again usually in the autumn months. Even if the lunar eclipse cannot be seen where you live, the energy of the eclipse spreads across the earth regardless.

During an eclipse, the magical correspondences change slightly to accommodate the darker elements of this time.

Eclipse Counteracting Energy Candles Spell

Moon Phase: Eclipse, and one week after the eclipse
Need: One black and one white tealight candle

Eclipses are one area where colour is especially significant within magic; the power of eclipses signifies a duality of black and white. Eclipses are notoriously revered in the magical world given their power to bring destructive change in both lives and society.

Counteract this negativity by representing both dark and light on your altar or in magical practice. On your altar, have a black candle and a white one or have a candle that represents the duality of this time. The shadow passing over a light source is temporary, but while it happens, light your candles and say this spell during the eclipse:

Black and white.
Day and night.
Chase darkness from my sight.
Moon return and beam your light.

The effects of the eclipse can be experienced a couple of days before the actual eclipse and then for several days after, so keep lighting your eclipse candles.

EQUINOX ENERGY

The equinox is a time when the sun and the moon have almost equal hours of the day and night as the earth turns; these are regarded as highly auspicious days, and we only have two of them each year, so make the most of them.

We have two equinoxes in our year. One of them is in spring and is often called the vernal equinox. If you are in the northern hemisphere, this happens between March 19 and 21. The other is in autumn and is simply called the

autumnal equinox. If you are in the northern hemisphere, this occurs between September 21 and 24. If you live in the southern hemisphere, the equinoxes are reversed, with the spring occurrence being in September and the autumnal one in March.

Equinox Salt

Moon Phase: Equinox
Need: Salt, dish

Use the power of the equinox to make a supercharged equinox salt. Simply leave your salt in a dish on a windowsill or outside (if it isn't raining) on the day of the equinox to charge. This salt can be used in all manner of things, from cooking to creating magical water that destroys all negative energies. Add three teaspoons to a spray bottle of water and shake up. Spray around you or anywhere you feel negative energy. Plus, use it for general cleansing.

Clean the house just as you would in spring. Clean the magic cupboard and sort out dried herbs and spices; toss anything out of date. With herbs and spices, sprinkle them on the garden, giving thanks for their power.

Moon Correspondences

Magical correspondences work off the idea that everything in this world is connected or related. Think of the universe as a giant spiderweb or net; by tugging one strand, you are triggering the others, which then pull that desired object or result to you. Just as the moon triggers the tides through an unseen physical force, the same effect occurs with correspondences.[41]

Everything within the universe is connected—planets, days of the week, the moon and the sun, plants, oils, colours,

41. See Moon Correspondence Chart in appendix.

and even feelings. As our technology advances and our knowledge of the world develops, the correspondences grow. For example, in the ancient world, scrying or seeing into the future was performed by looking into a piece of obsidian—usually a black obsidian bowl filled with water. We can now use the shiny black surface of our laptops, phones, and flat-screen TVs to scry. Just as our knowledge evolves, so do the correspondences, and we can tap into these at any time.

Here, we are going to look at the moon's transferable power to water, salt, moonstone, moon herbs, and flowers, and how to capture that power for use in our magical practice.

MOON WATER

Moon water is a powerful resource to have in your magical supplies. You don't need gallons of it; a little bottle or mason jar will suffice. When making it, simply fill a clean jar or jug with tap water (you may use mineral water if you wish, but there really is no need). Leave it in full view of a full moon all night. In the morning, safely pour it into a bottle or place the lid on the jar. Label and date the bottle with the name of the moon it falls under, such as Straw-

berry Moon or Harvest Moon. Use the water as and when needed, in absolutely everything. Here is an example of a spell using moon water.

Moon Water Energy Shift Bath Spell

Moon Phase: Any
Need: Moon water, moon salt (see page 108), moon essential oils (see page 106)

On the night of the full moon, run a warm bath and add some moon salt and the moon essential oil of your choice. Pour your moon water in and swish the water with your hand before you enter the bath. As you do, say this spell:

> *Healing waters of the moon.*
> *Sea of Storms and Tranquillity.*
> *I surrender to the Sea of Serenity.*
> *Renew my power and energy.*

Relax in the bath and imagine you are floating up to the moon. Feel the weightlessness of the water and visualise the mystical waters healing and energising you.

MOON OIL

Unlike moon water, which is very cheap to make, moon oil is not, depending on where you live, as moon oil requires the best olive oil available. Extra-virgin olive oil is best, and for moon oil, there are no substitutes, so do not use sunflower or rapeseed as this will not cut it with the gods and especially not with the moon. If you do try to cut corners, the spells and magical intentions will likely backfire. You have been warned.

Buy a small bottle of olive oil. Do not open it, but clean and wash the outside of the bottle to remove the labels, leaving a clean, unopened bottle of olive oil. Leave it out in full view of the full moon. Because it is unopened, you can leave it outside as nothing can crawl into it. Leave it out all night; in the morning, label and date it as with the moon water.

This moon oil can now be used for absolutely everything from cooking to consecration, spells, brews, anointings, and massage. When using it in cooking, do not use the entire bottle due to its value; I tend to use three to five drops of it, and then I add the less expensive oil for the rest of the cooking.

Essential oils can also benefit from an infusion of moon energy. Essential oils come in a plethora of scents, from flowers to herbs, spices, and trees—tea tree, pine, and eucalyptus are very popular. These oils are the concentrated plant or tree oil, so always use wisely, and never apply directly to the skin. They are usually very expensive, so use sparingly in your magic, and gradually build up a collection of the most commonly used ones.

Generally, essential oils are used for massage, consecration, and purifying, and they have found their way into beauty products, including shampoos, conditioners, and shower gels.

Leave the bottle out in full view of the full moon just as with your olive oil. In the morning, store it safely away in a dark place as many essential oils lose their potency if left in the light for too long. Every couple of months, recharge the oil by leaving it out on a full moon and use as needed in your magic or beauty regimes.

Moon Oil and Water Friendship Spell

Moon Phase: Any
Need: Olive oil, water, bowl

If you have had a falling-out with your friend or have a colleague you cannot get along with but now must work with, try an oil and water spell. Pour some moon water into a bowl and add a couple of drops of your moon oil. Using your right index finger, stir the water and oil clockwise. As you do, say these words:

> *Oil and water do not mix; this friendship I must fix.*
> *Enemies from days of yore,*
> *Our friendship to mend will last forevermore.*

Close your eyes and think of your friend or colleague. Think about how you could be friends and imagine you're having fun and working together.

MOON SALT

This is a firm favourite of mine and one you simply cannot be without. Just like olive oil, it can be used in absolutely everything for every single imaginable reason, and not just magical. Making it is very easy, but once again, try not to cut corners with the salt. The best salt to use is sea salt, Himalayan rock salt (usually pink), Hawaiian black lava salt, or any other salt that is pure as can be. I do have a range of salts in all the varied colours for all different intentions and uses, but you can start with one.

Leave the salt out on the night of the full moon in a dish or bowl. Leave overnight in the moon's rays. In the morning, place in an airtight container; always use a glass container, never plastic, as plastic can diminish the salt's power quickly. Label and date the jar, including the moon type (Blood Moon, Cold Moon, etc.).

Moon Salt Cleaning Power Spell

Moon Phase: Any

Need: Moon water, moon salt, lemon slice, spray bottle

On a warm moonlit evening, clean out your wardrobes and wash blankets, sweaters, and winter coats or summer dresses to get ready for the coming season. Anything you haven't worn this year, put it in a charity bag or sell it online.

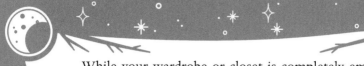

While your wardrobe or closet is completely empty, cleanse it with moon water, salt, and a couple of lemon slices in a spray bottle. Spritz and wipe down with moon power. As you're cleaning, say,

> *Fresh and clean with moon energy,*
> *Make sure all my clothes still fit me.*
> *The moon changes quick and fast,*
> *Cleansing this wardrobe with clothes of the past.*

If you have a chest of drawers, repeat the process and spell. Completely utilise the moon's powers to bring in cleaning and cleansing energies of renewal.

MOON SUGAR

Moon sugar is another powerful ingredient that can be used in absolutely everything. I tend to amplify the energy of the sugar by adding herbs, flowers, plants, or tree bits. For example, if I am baking moon cakes for Yule, I will use pine sugar—sugar infused with pine leaves. Simply collect some fresh pine leaves, wash them under warm running water, and leave them to dry. When completely dry, leave them in your jar of sugar, then leave the jar in the glare of the full moon. Always label and date your sugar. Here is a sample spell using moon sugar:

Moon Sugar Beauty Scrub
Moon Phase: Any
Need: Moon sugar, oatmeal, organic yogurt, honey

Beauty is not just about the surface, but the actual depth and beauty of a person's soul. What you put inside is just as important as what you put on the outside. Always try to use the purest and most natural products for your largest organ: your skin.

This mask is simple to make and suitable for all skin types as it cleanses and rejuvenates. Use one tablespoon of oatmeal, finely ground, one tablespoon of plain organic yogurt, one tablespoon of moon sugar, and a teaspoon of honey. Dump the ingredients into a small bowl, fold in, and mix well. As you stir, say these words:

> *Face mask, beautify me.*
> *Release my inner beauty.*

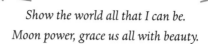

Show the world all that I can be.
Moon power, grace us all with beauty.

Apply the mask to the face and neck and décolletage for about ten minutes before washing off with warm water and applying your moisturiser as normal.

Moon Power Ritual Body Scrub

Ritual body scrubs are perfect when ridding oneself of all the negative toxins we accumulate throughout the week. This one infuses with the energy of the moon and creates a balancing and harmonising body scrub.

Use a half cup of moon sugar, a half cup of finely ground Himalayan or sea salt, a half cup of coconut oil, ten drops each of jojoba, sweet almond, evening primrose, and wheatgerm essential oils. Mix well before storing in a glass jar and label Moon Power Body Scrub. Use when you are about to perform a ritual for the moon or any other magical work. Apply to wet skin after you've washed, working your hands in a slow, circular motion, and think about the movement of the moon when massaging into the skin. Rinse off and pat your body dry.

Crystals and Herbs

Crystals and herbs are often used with the moon's energy to enhance and amplify magic and affirmations.

PLANTS AND HERBS

There are many plants and herbs directly associated with the moon, and many are connected to female energy. They are often cleansing and spiritually healing plants with powerful benefits, so use sparingly in your magical practice. These plants correspond to the moon via their presence within the feminine divine and represent both the moon

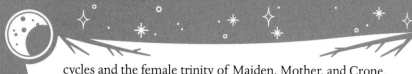

cycles and the female trinity of Maiden, Mother, and Crone. These plants can help with menstrual cramps, ease hormonal conditions, or give welcomed natural pain relief during labour.

Blue Lotus

Nymphaea caerulea

Moon Phase: Waning, Dark Moon
Divine Femina: Crone

The blue lotus is an Egyptian water lily; many tombs and relics of ancient Egypt have highly decorated images of the water lily. It has been used throughout the centuries in medicinal recipes for pain relief and neurological disorders. It was also used in religious rituals as it contains a psychoactive alkaloid that can produce gentle euphoric states.

In many aromatherapy practices, the blue lotus gives complete relaxation to the individual. When combined with the power of the moon, this little flower can become incredibly potent with sensual energy and passion.

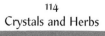

Fennel

Foeniculum vulgare

Moon Phase: New Moon
Divine Femina: Maiden

Fennel is rich in phytoestrogens and therefore is often used in female herbal remedies. It helps with breast enlargement, promoting menstruation, amenorrhea, suppressing appetite, improving digestion, milk flow, and increasing urine flow. Fennel is extremely beneficial for many digestive disorders, including colic, wind, irritable bowel syndrome, and water retention. It is also used to boost sexual desire and the libido.

The moon enhances the power of this herb in spells regarding confidence and courage. Given its medicinal properties for the sexual health of women, fennel is also good for fertility spells and those magical practices regarding love, lust, and sex. Fennel can also be used for psychic protection, divination, and purification.

Hibiscus

Malvaceae

Moon Phase: New Moon

Divine Femina: Maiden

Hibiscus is a beautiful, exotic plant that traditionally grows in tropical regions. It has been used most notably in teas and drinks and in folk medicine as its vitamin C content lowers high blood pressure. This plant is estrogenic; it is advised that pregnant women and those who are breastfeeding do not take hibiscus in any form as it can stimulate menstruation.

Milk Thistle

Silybum marianum

Moon Phase: Full Moon

Divine Femina: Mother

Milk thistle is renowned for cleansing and promoting a healthy liver. Its detoxifying attributes are second to none, and many reach for it over the holiday period if they have overdone the alcohol and rich food. Milk thistle can also be

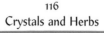

used to manage cholesterol, diabetes, heartburn, and menstrual pain.

Thistle has been used for thousands of years for its medicinal properties. Milk thistle is used to heal and restore the liver. It is often used for the treatment of liver disease and for the prevention and treatment of cancer. It is also an ideal supportive treatment for death cap mushroom poisoning.

Magically, thistles have long been used by practitioners for various correspondences, most notably for protection, energy, and happiness. It is an herb that comes under the goddess Hecate's watchful gaze, which provides protection from lightening. Today, many people wear a thistle for protection from evil and negativity. It is often used as a purification resource and as a hex-breaking plant, for which it is very powerful.

Rose

Rosaceae

Moon Phase: Waxing, Full Moon

Divine Femina: Mother

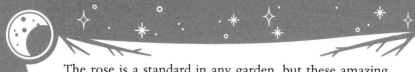

The rose is a standard in any garden, but these amazing flowers stem from the wild rose or dog rose. Rose hip syrup is used to treat chest complaints and ease the symptoms of the common cold. Rose hip syrup is packed with vitamin C and contains 20 percent more of this immune-boosting vitamin than oranges. The rose hips themselves contain not only vitamin C but also flavonoids, tannins, and many other vitamins. Rose has sedative and antidepressant properties, is astringent, and is useful for lowering cholesterol. Rose vinegar can be used to cure headaches.

Rose is probably one of the most common resources we have for love magic—rose petals, rose oil, or even rose quartz is always used in some way when a practitioner is performing a love spell or ritual.

This beautiful little flower can also be used to raise divinatory energies, unveil mysteries, provide protection, and increase healing. Rose is good to use when contacting the Fae or other elemental beings of the woodland and forests, especially if the rose is the wild rose or dog rose. Rose is ideal as an offering or gift to fairies and nymphs, and mermaids are rather partial to the wild rose, viewing it as a unique gift; the fragrance and texture appeal to the watery world of the merfolk, especially on a full moon. However, elves do not appreciate the rose and prefer more earthy gifts of trees, moss, or woodland herbs.

Sage

Salvia sclarea

Moon Phase: Waning, Dark Moon

Divine Femina: Crone

A firm favourite of many practitioners of moon magic and magic in general. Garden sage is one of the go-to herbs we have for all menstrual conditions, including the symptoms of perimenopause and menopause, and as such sage is often called the Crone's herb. Sage can also help with stomach upsets, kidney diseases, anxiety, and stress. Sage has many health benefits and was one of the primary medicinal herbs of our ancestors. Its antiseptic action is of value where there is intestinal infection. Further, it also reduces muscle tension. Sage has an antispasmodic action that reduces tension in smooth muscle, and it can be used in a steam inhalation for asthma attacks. It is an excellent remedy for removing mucous congestion in the airways and for check-ing or preventing secondary infection.

Sage is one of those truly magical and all-round herbs that can be used for everything, whether physical, emo-tional, psychological, or spiritual. One of the most common and ancient magical practices involving sage is, of course, its use in incense sticks for cleansing, purification, detoxify-ing the environment, and protection. Sage has been used in this way for centuries by the Indigenous peoples of North and South America. Sage has been used since ancient times to bring good luck and promote wisdom. It is great for pro-tection spells and is also used to grant wishes, especially when used in conjunction with the power of a full moon.

CRYSTALS

Like plants, crystals also respond to the moon's energy and power. Generally, all crystals benefit from being bathed, cleansed, and consecrated in the full moon's light. It reen-ergises them, removes unneeded energy, and charges their powerful spiritual batteries.

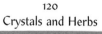

One stone that is deeply connected to the moon is the moonstone, of course. This powerful stone can be used for all manner of healing and divinatory practices. I have a set of runes made from moonstone, and they resonate a unique energy. Along with moonstone, here are the main moon crystals I tend to use.

Moonstone

Moon Phase: Any
Divinity: Gender Neutral

The moonstone can come in a range of colours—from a pure white to a cream to an almost peachy-yellow colour—and have a translucent quality. They are quite common and can be easily found in many New Age and crystal shops. Moonstone can be used in magic working specifically with the moon. If you do have a moonstone, bathe it at least once a month in the full moon's light. Leave it out overnight to help it recharge.

Rainbow Moonstone
Moon Phase: Any
Divinity: LGBTQIA+

Rainbow moonstone can be used for all manner of things. Its base colour is white, but inside, in an opalescent way, it shimmers with all the colours of the rainbow, hence its name. It is particularly potent for securing friendships, helping with understanding, and romance for all my beautiful friends who are LGBTQIA+. A stunning stone to look at and to use in an array of magical intentions, including working with elementals of the sky (angels, griffins, and the Pegasus).

Black Moonstone
Moon Phase: Full Moon or Dark Nights
Divinity: Gender Neutral

I love to use black moonstone for negative feelings, such as lack of confidence, loneliness, lack of self-worth, or simply for tiredness. I tend to drop a black moonstone in the bath when I'm really stressed along with a couple of tablespoons

of moon salt. Simply soak in the water and let the powers of moon and rock do their work.

Selenite
Moon Phase: New / Crescent Moon Waxing or Waning
Divinity: Gender Neutral

Selenite crystals come in an array of shapes and sizes—wands, towers, and spheres—and they look stunning in every form. Selenite comes in a pearly white colour, and although it is named after the ancient Greek moon goddess Selene, it is gender neutral, as many crystals are. Selenite can be used to clear thoughts and consciousness in preparation for revising for an exam, allowing you to focus your mind more clearly. Leave it on your desk or books as you study and occasionally hold it in both hands when you take a break.

Charging Crystals Spell
It is advisable to charge your crystals at least twice a year by the light of the full moon. Charging crystals is not the same as cleansing them. Charging crystals means reenergising

with the power of the moon so they are working at their optimum crystal level.

Moon Phase: Full Moon
Need: Crystals, water, incense

To charge your crystals, begin by cleaning them under running water or wafting incense over them if they are water soluble. After, set to one side and leave to dry in the air. On a window ledge or outside in the garden, leave your crystal in the moon's rays. Hold your arms up toward the moon and say these words:

> *Goddess of glory light,*
> *Recharge my crystals this night.*
> *Harness the power and the might,*
> *To carry on in day's sight.*

Leave the crystals in the moon's light. In the morning, carefully store as usual. Some crystals need to be stored out of sight and only used for specific occasions.

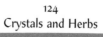

Magical Phases

The moon has four primary phases—first quarter, full moon, last quarter, and new moon—and four intermediate phases, which are the waxing and waning of the moon. Here, I have concentrated on the actual phases and have not gone into detail regarding all the different quarters. In magic, whatever part the moon is waning or waxing in—first quarter, third quarter, etc.—the emphasis is on what it brings and the magical preference it has, not the particular stage the moon is at in its development within the month.

The moon's cycle begins with the dark moon, of which there are three nights. The moon is hidden from our sights until, finally, we see a slight sliver of silver light in the shape of a crescent moon. Though the dark moon phase is the

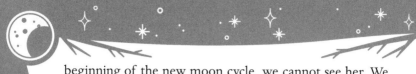

beginning of the new moon cycle, we cannot see her. We then have the new moon phase before it turns to the waxing crescent, and on to the first quarter and then the waxing gibbous, which leads to the full moon. After the three nights of the full moon, the moon begins its decent by waning or shrinking. The first phase in this cycle is waning gibbous, which then turns to the last quarter, and finally to the waning crescent. The moon then disappears from sight to begin the process again.

Each phase brings its own magical specialisms and emphasises every aspect of human life, and by learning these, we can tune our lives in to working in harmony with the moon. You can use these spells and charms during whatever stage the moon is at in the month. For example, waxing crescent or waxing first quarter are both good for spells and magical intent on increasing something or drawing health, wealth, or love to you.

In each phase, I provide an example ritual pertaining to that specific moon phase. Rituals are incredibly individual, and many practitioners will have a ritualistic bath or shower

before they commence. This is to cleanse themselves of the day's influence and to get rid of any negative toxins they may have encountered. You may like to follow these rituals or to create your own designed for your own needs. All these rituals have been written with a moon altar in mind, but you do not have to follow that practice; you may have created something else, such as a shelf or even a room, where you feel comfortable performing magic.

DARK MOON

The dark moon is that time when we cannot see the moon; it lasts for three whole nights as the moon goes through her cycles before we see that tiny sliver of a shiny crescent moon. These dark nights when the light of the moon is nowhere to be seen must have been so frightening to our ancestors. However, it became a time of prophesising and seeing into the darkness. We have carried this tradition through to present day, and the emphasis of this phase is all about seeing into the dark and viewing the unknown.

Dark Moon Ritual

Need: Black candle, patchouli incense, a few pinches of belladonna

Place the black candle, patchouli incense, and a few pinches of belladonna in a dish on your altar. On the dark moon night, weather permitting, go outside, raise your arms to the night skies, and say,

> *Glory of the Dark Moon, I call to thee.*
> *I seek your power and into the unknown I will see.*
> *Round and round in darkness and depth,*
> *Upon your eternal night I will tread.*
> *Dark Moon rising, blackness on high.*
> *Welcome to you upon this night.*

Embrace the night sky and the dark; welcome them into your arms and heart and feel the connection with the moon's dark side, which is always there, and not just on nights when we do not see the moon. Stay for some time outside, embracing the night, and when you feel your welcome ritual is finished, bow to the sky and say thank you.

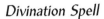

Divination Spell

Moon Phase: Any of the three nights when the moon does not appear

Need: Tarot/oracle cards, different coloured ribbons, candles, bowl of water, runes, and other divinatory resources you feel akin to

Divination is something we all can do; it's just a case of finding the right form of divination that works for you. There are so many different forms, from tarot and oracle cards to flower reading, ribbon reading, or scrying, which is looking into a bowl of water or candle flame to see the future. Every culture has some form of divination; from Celtic divination to numerology, there are many different forms. If you are unsure, perform a divination spell to see what your soul resonates with.

On the night of the dark moon, have a selection of divination products from all different types. You can use pictures of them before you buy them to save time and money.

Have pictures or the product itself (tarot cards, oracle cards, ribbons, crystals, tea, coffee, numbers, dice, dowsing

rods, pendulum, and scrying bowls) laid out in a straight row on a table or flat surface. For scrying bowls, which are usually black obsidian, you can scry from your black phone or laptop screen. Give your hands a good shake, and then say,

> *In the darkness let me see,*
> *With vision and clarity.*
> *What I choose by me is right,*
> *As I divine within the light.*

Close your hands and slowly move them over the row of pictures and objects. Do not touch them. When your fingertips or palms start to tingle or feel hot, stop, and open your eyes. Remove that particular picture or object to one side, then continue. You may have four or five that feel right to you as you move your hands over the objects.

When you no longer feel as though anything is speaking to you, remove the other objects from the table. Repeat the process with the other objects until you get down to about two or three divinatory products and begin to research and use them. Utilise the dark moon and start to practice and use the tools throughout this phase.

Hex-Breaking Brew

If you feel you have been hexed and nothing seems to be going right for you, utilise the dark moon by making a hex-breaking brew.

Moon Phase: Dark Moon
Need:

1 cup water
1 apple, thinly sliced horizontally, exposing the
    pentagram inside
1 onion, thinly chopped
3 pinches moon salt
1 tablespoon honey
1 star anise

Put all ingredients in a saucepan and bring to a boil. Simmer for thirty minutes. Stir widdershins for the final ten minutes. As you stir, say these words over the brew:

> *Wax and wane,*
> *Receive no pain.*
> *Wane and wax,*
> *Return this hex.*

No more hurt.
No more love.
Now only grace from above.
Dark Moon power released in this hour,
Return this hex to the sender.
This hex is at an ender.

Remove from heat and allow to cool. When it is warm, drink an egg cupful to break the hex. Afterward, bottle it up in a glass jar, and make sure to label and date the brew. After the month has gone and the hex has lifted because good luck has returned, scatter the remaining brew on the garden or outside.

NEW MOON

In the ancient world, the new moon was often revered as a sign of renewed hope and a chance at a new beginning. The symbol of the new moon featured in many tombs and temples as it epitomized a new life emerging as the soul transitioned into the next stage of life. Today, the new moon still holds power for many, and there are superstitions galore during the first night of a new moon, such as turning your money in hope that more will come throughout the month. The new moon is also a perfect time to draw a new love into your life or reignite an old relationship.

New Moon Ritual

Need: Yellow candle, a lemon, a daffodil plant in a bowl or freshly cut daffodils

Place the yellow candle, a lemon, and the daffodils (or any yellow flowers you're growing) in a bowl on your altar (you can also use lemon balm leaves or dill if you haven't any flowers).

The new moon brings so much new energy and bountiful gifts of starting over. A new moon is like a new slate, and you can start a new month with a new purpose. Acknowledge this potential in your new moon ritual as you welcome its return.

On the night of the new moon, go outside, weather permitting, light a brand-new yellow candle, and hold it in both your hands, slightly raised to the sky. Say,

New Moon on the horizon, lighting up the night sky,
I welcome your presence in my life.

You are blessed on your return.
I am grateful to all the goodness you bring.
New Moon of life and love, sending grace from above,
Let all my ventures this month be blessed.
Let projects be completed, may deadlines be met.
Let love renew and friendship progress.
I welcome you, New Moon, into my life.

Meditate on the light of the new moon. In your mind, go through all your plans for this month and feel the moon's strength flow into you, renewing your enthusiasm for tasks and projects that need to be completed. When the candle blows itself out, that is the end of your ritual. Give thanks to the new moon and bow as you walk away.

New Beginnings Spell

Moon Phase: New Moon
Need: Yellow tealight candle, clean glass jar, dillseed, lemon balm, moonstone, yellow rose petals

A new beginning is a wonderful feeling, especially if it is something you have instigated yourself. It is a chance to start over and put all your magical energy into whatever is a new start for you. It could be a new job, a new project, a new place to live, a new hobby—anything at all could be new. Channel the new moon energies into a new beginnings jar to keep you safe and positive on your new venture.

On the night of a new moon, light a yellow candle. In a clean glass jar, place dill seed, lemon balm, a small piece of moonstone, and yellow rose petals. Place the lid on the top. As you do, say,

> *Time will only tell, but a new beginning for me.*
> *New Moon blessings bring good times and energy.*
> *From now until a month's end, let this jar bring positivity.*

Sit holding your new beginnings jar for some time while thinking of all the projects or new beginnings you have. Then place your jar in the light of the new moon and leave overnight. Safely extinguish the candle.

In the morning, place your jar on your altar or somewhere you will see it every day. If throughout the month you are worried or concerned you've made a bad decision

regarding your new beginning, hold the jar in both hands for a while and give it a little shake to reactivate the positivity.

Positivity and Happiness Spell

Moon Phase: New Moon

Need: Cardboard, paper, photographs, colouring pens/ pencils

There are certain times in our life when positivity and happiness escape us, and we find it difficult to think of positive things. Even laughing at something seems to elude us. When we are bursting with happiness, we are full of positive thoughts, and we feel invincible. If you have been feeling rather down lately, use the power of the new moon and change the energies.

On the night of a new moon, create a mood board of happiness and positivity. On a large piece of paper, draw a happy and smiling new moon. Do not worry that it's not perfect—what is? Draw the crescent shape with a smile and big eyes; you can colour it in if you want. Around the moon, write what makes you happy. Look for pictures that make you laugh, or photographs taken at a happy time.

Remember the bountiful positivity you felt during these times and place it all over your board. As you hang your board on the wall, say these words:

Bless this board with happy positivity.
Every time I look at it, may a smile beam from my face.
May this shine like a new moon and bring
Happy positivity all over the place.

Keep your happy new moon board up all month or for as long as you need it. Each new moon, you could add new pictures of positivity to it, such as a good grade or a photo of friends—anything that makes you feel happy and bursting with positivity.

WAXING MOON

The waxing moon is the phase during which the moon is growing and increasing; think of it as coming toward you. This phase is commonly used for pulling money and physical things toward you, such as a new car or the right house. Use this phase when you want to draw something toward you throughout the month.

Waxing Moon Ritual

Need: Rose, red candle, sprigs of rosemary, an image of
something you want to increase, deity representation (if
you follow the gods) or an image of the moon, moon
journal, pen

Place the listed items on your altar to focus your intent. Get
your moon journal and pen.

On the night of a waxing moon, sit or kneel in front of
the altar and light your candle. Raise your palms out as if to
receive and say,

Blessed Waxing Moon, welcome.
Bring your strength and power with you, and may it always follow
me wherever I go.
I welcome your energies into my life and into my home.
Grant me the changes that only you can bring,
And may I be worthy of all the gifts you send.

Meditate for some time, thinking about the waxing
moon and the energies she is bringing toward you. Keep
the candle burning for as long as possible—little tealights

are quite handy for altar candles as they burn themselves out, but never leave a lit candle unattended. When you are ready, offer thanks to the waxing moon and safely extinguish the candle.

Money Drawing Spell

Moon Phase: Always waxing moon when drawing anything, especially money, to you

Need: Green tealight candle

We all could do with a bit of extra money now and then, and the best moon phase to cast a money spell is when the moon is waxing. This powerful energy of pulling something toward you is crucial when it comes to drawing in more money during the month.

Light a green candle and waft your hands around the flame carefully, not too close, as if to draw the light toward you. Then say three times,

> *I draw to you as you draw to me.*
> *I am drawing money, money, money.*
> *Increase this amount three times three.*

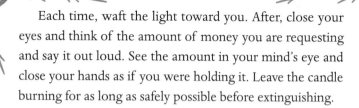

Each time, waft the light toward you. After, close your eyes and think of the amount of money you are requesting and say it out loud. See the amount in your mind's eye and close your hands as if you were holding it. Leave the candle burning for as long as safely possible before extinguishing.

Developing Talent Spell
Moon Phase: Waxing Moon
Need: Moon salt, paper, pen, one red tealight candle

As a teacher, I am a firm believer that everyone is good at least with one thing, and this is a gift from the universe and should not be wasted. The gift is your natural talent, and it can be in absolutely anything and everything, from singing, dancing, or sports to spelling any word or seeing the answers to equations and puzzles. We often do not realise we have a talent as perhaps we were taught as children it did not mean anything. We may not realise our gift is a talent because it comes so easy to us, and that is the telling case of a talent—it comes naturally, it's easy to do, we enjoy it, and whatever it is, we do it really well.

However, as with most things, we have to nurture it and give it time. We may need training to discipline ourselves in our natural talent, but whatever it is we are good at and enjoy, we have to let it develop.

On the night of a waxing moon, light a red candle and write down your talent and what you think you are good at. Sprinkle three pinches of moon salt over it and place both your hands on the paper. Say,

> *There is something I am working on.*
> *A gift, a talent, in which I am strong.*
> *Let it grow and develop more.*
> *Waxing Moon, grant this and more.*

Carefully fold up the paper with the salt inside and close your eyes. Imagine your talent developing and the potential career path it could take you down. Whatever your talent, look into development, such as training or going back to school. After you have visualised your developing talent, safely extinguish the candle and keep the folded paper in a safe place where only you can find it.

WANING MOON

Many practitioners do not like a waning moon as it often brings a loss with it, and sometimes this can be incredibly painful, but loss can also be a gain, and we need to experience both in order to grow. A waning moon is a perfect time to cast spells when you are ridding something you no longer wish to have in your life or heart. This is an ideal time to create banishing spells or cut the cord between someone or something that has run its course for you but is still attached to you and draining your energy.

Waning Moon Ritual

Need: Green candle, a few sprigs of mint, cedar oil, an English ivy plant, a picture of something you want to rid yourself of this month, a dish of salt

Place the listed items on your altar. Light the green candle and have your arms out front, your palms facing the ground. Take a few deep breaths and say,

> *Waning Moon, I embrace thee for all the good you do,*
> *For all the cleansing and taking away of negativity.*

Remove all things from my path that no longer serve me.
Waning Moon, you are neither wrong nor right.
After all, you still light the way on dark nights.
Waning Moon, I welcome you into my life and home.

Take four pinches of the salt and scatter each pinch around you from side to side; this is to cleanse the area as a waning moon can take away negativity. Think of the salt as purifying the spiritual space around you. Meditate on the things you want to get rid of this moon phase. Leave the candle burning for as long as possible; once again, a little green tealight is ideal for altar candles. Safely extinguish.

Weight Loss Spell
Moon Phase: Waning
Need: Moon journal, green tealight candle

A waning moon is a perfect time to instigate a weight loss program. In your moon journal, draw three columns. In the first column, write what you weigh now. Be honest with yourself and put how much you really weigh. In the next column, put how much you should weigh. In the final column,

put how much you need to lose. Keep the page open in front of your altar or wherever you do your magic and light a green candle. Place your left hand on the page and say,

> *Take away this overeat.*
> *Take away this extra meat.*
> *No more takeaway.*
> *I will diet every day.*

For the next month, halve what you eat and try to move or exercise every single day. Alternate your exercise (try walking, then maybe swimming, and then perhaps cycle to work). If you feel like snacking and hitting the chocolate bar instead of an exercise bar, go outside and stare at the moon until the moment passes. Every time you feel yourself slipping, go outside and look at the moon, for she is with you on your journey. Each month during a waning moon, repeat the spell until you have achieved your goal weight.

Moving Spell
Moon Phase: Waning
Need: Memories

Moving house is one of the most stressful things to do along with death and divorce, all of which require leaving. Many people fear the moving aspect due to the amount of change and upheaval experienced, but it does not have to be feared. Embrace that change and look upon it as a new opportunity and a new beginning for yourself.

If you are moving home and you are packing, cast this spell on the waning moon to help your anxieties for the future, but also to say goodbye. Walk from room to room and say,

> *I am moving and leaving now.*
> *This house was my home, my sanctuary.*
> *But now I am moving somewhere new.*
> *But I will always remember you.*
> *I will embrace the new changes coming my way.*
> *I will go forward into a bright new day.*

Spend a few moments in each room thinking about all the good times you had there before visualising your new place and all its potential. After, physically say goodbye in each room, then continue packing, and gradually feel better about moving.

GIBBOUS MOON

The gibbous moon is when the moon is either convex or swelling and literally means "small hump." It appears just before the full moon and right after; check a moon chart if you are unsure if it's waxing or waning. The gibbous moon energy when it is leading to the full moon is very similar to a waxing moon; the waxing moon phase is a subtle phase of growth and gradually increasing power, and the gibbous moon is an explosion of growth. The gibbous moon comes in with the same amount of energy and expansion as a solar flare eruption. This is the phase in which spells cast are almost instantaneous in their impact and result. Similarly, when the gibbous moon is waning, it brings a swift decrease in something, so be careful casting on a waning gibbous.

Gibbous Moon Ritual

Need: Blue candle, salt, lavender, hyssop, morning glory (plants, flowers, oils, or incense)

On the night of a gibbous moon, go outside and scatter salt in the biggest circle you can in the space you have. Make sure you are standing in the circle as you make it; walk around deosil, scattering the salt. In the centre, raise your arms to the moon and say,

Welcome Gibbous Moon of growth and expansion.
May all my magical workings
this phase be as big and as wonderful as you.
I can see your strength as you grow and realise how far I can go.
I welcome you; I embrace you.
Grant me the secrets to success in this phase.
Blessings to all in this place.

Sit for a while in your circle and look at the moon. If you have a telescope, this is a good time to use it to view the gibbous moon. See the potential for major work during this expansive time. After, break your circle by saying these words as you brush the salt away:

Scattering to the winds,
Seeping through the earth.

> *No more circle, no more ritual.*
> *Now only moon magic's birth.*

Go about your evening or utilise the gibbous moon by performing specific spells that require its particular type of energy.

Growth Spell

Moon Phase: Waxing Gibbous
Need: Lavender plant, pen, paper

If there is something you are trying to grow either in the garden or in business and it's just not expanding the way you want it to, ask the gibbous moon for some help.

On the night of a gibbous moon, plant a lavender bush, no matter how small. If you do not have a garden, buy a small lavender plant and keep it in the home on a window ledge. Transfer it into a larger pot and write what you wish to expand on a small piece of paper. Place the paper in the pot or garden and cover with soil. Say,

Gibbous Moon, I beseech your power and your growth.
Expand my business/garden with bountiful acclaim.
I nurture all in your name.

Lovingly tend to your garden and lavender plant and the gibbous moon will tend to your business or whatever it is you wish to grow.

Sharing Together Charm
Moon Phase: Waning Gibbous
Need: Photos, blue ribbon, sprig of lavender

This is a good charm to make during the gibbous moon, especially if there are siblings who constantly fight and bicker and will not share toys, clothes, or the car.

On the night of the gibbous moon, have two photos of the people who cannot share and wrap the photos together with a piece of blue ribbon. As you do, say,

Better together, sharing forever.
Take away this bickering forever.

When you have tied the photos together, place a little sprig of lavender in the middle of the charm and hang it up in a place where the people in the photo will usually start fighting. If it's at work, keep your charm safely in your drawer.

The Full Moon

The full moon is the phase that most people associate with magic. During our moon's phases, we may lose her for three dark nights, but then we gain her shine in full bloom for three. The three nights are significant in magic as they are utilised for all manner of intents and spells, from manifestation to healing and weaving spells. The full moon is also the time when we can see some wonderful sights, especially as it rises or sets throughout the year.

THE MOON AND ITS COLOURS

One of these sights is the colour of the moon. The names we have given our moon throughout the centuries is due in part to the colour it appears as it is rising and reflecting

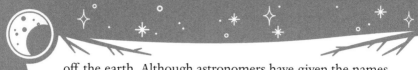

off the earth. Although astronomers have given the names of blue and black to the moon due to its reappearance or nonappearance in a month, it does not commonly appear as these colours, unfortunately. Meanwhile, the names pink, yellow, and orange moon have found their way into the general language with many using these terms when a certain moon colour is predicted. Around the world, many news reporters will discuss the colour of a predicted moon at the end of a programme for that homely sound bite while not necessarily realising the magical or historical importance of the terms.

The moon's transferable power can be utilised for all manner of needs, such as love, romance, health, and education, and its effects are amplified by its colour. These moons may not necessarily glow the bright colours you immediately imagine (although yellow and orange moons do appear vividly, usually in the beginning of the evening as the moon rises on the horizon). These moons of many colours can occur at any time throughout the year, and some of them are extremely rare, such as the black or blue moons. Others can and will be experienced throughout the year.

Pink Moon

Correspondences: Love, romance, friendship, marriage

The pink moon is usually associated with a supermoon, which makes the moon look closer to the earth than normal. This happens when the moon is closest to the earth during its elliptical orbit. Supermoons can occur at any time; traditionally, the pink moon occurs in April, but some have started using the term throughout the year.

The pink moon brings with it the energies of love in its many forms, from lovers to friends to pets and even to the love of work and career.

Pink Moon Love Spell

Moon Phase: Full Moon
Need: Love

In a world of so many changes and broken promises, we may find it difficult to build a lasting relationship. We may become closed to other people and find it hard to express or

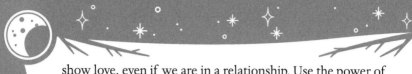

show love, even if we are in a relationship. Use the power of the pink moon to open your heart and express the love you feel for family, friends, and lovers.

During a pink moon, stand barefoot outside or in front of your indoor altar with your palms turned upward to receive love and say,

> *Increase my love,*
> *My capacity to give.*
> *I am ready to show love,*
> *From the grace up above.*
> *I open my heart and embrace.*
> *I will share my love all over the place.*

Stand for some time watching the moon, or if indoors, close your eyes and imagine a pink moon pouring pink water into you. Feel the warmth as it flows from your toes, feet, knees, thighs, and up to your heart and head, filling your whole body with love until you are glowing pink from inside.

Blue Moon

Correspondences: Health, mind, knowledge, education

The moon has found her way into our language, and we can refer to her in so many ways. One of my favourite sayings is "once in a blue moon," which means a very rare occurrence, as there is a blue moon every two or three years. The blue moon refers to the second full moon in any one month. Occasionally you will have two blue moons in one year, but this only happens every twenty-five years.

Because a blue moon is such a rare occurrence, it is very powerful. Making your magic moon salt becomes even more important as this salt is doubly charged with the power of the moon.

There are many reasons why it is called a blue moon, and at times, the moon does look blue. One of the main reasons is atmospheric interference—for example, after the volcanic eruption of Krakatoa in 1883, the dust particles caused the moon to appear blue for two years.

Blue Moon Healthcare Brew

Moon Phase: The second full moon of a month
Need: Coriander, fennel, honey, boiling water

The colour of blue and a blue moon have always been connected to the area of health. Whether it is the health of the mind, body, or soul, a blue moon amplifies the usual power of the moon, probably because it is the second full moon in a month. Utilise the healing energy by performing a general health spell.

In front of your altar, make an herbal tea of a teaspoon of coriander, a teaspoon of dried fennel, and honey to taste. Allow to steep in boiling water, stir the tea deosil (clockwise), and say,

> *Coriander and fennel cleansing me,*
> *Healing my heart, mind, and body.*
> *Blue Moon of healing, hear me please.*
> *Toxins and negativity within now release,*
> *From now until three days have passed.*
> *Blue Moon, heal me at last.*

For the three nights of the blue moon, drink the coriander and fennel tea; be sure to make a fresh batch every night.

Black Moon

Correspondences: Protection, opportunity, enterprise, power

There are three meanings for a black moon. One is when there is an absence of a full moon in a month, which, given the shortage of days, usually occurs in February, but this is such a rare event—it only happens every nineteen years.

The other descriptions of a black moon relate to the new moon of a month. One of them refers to a month with no new moon. Once again, this is extremely rare, occurring every nineteen years, and it can happen in any month.

The most common meaning for the black moon is the flip side of a blue moon, but relates to the new moon appearing twice in one month. This is a very rare event and usually happens once every two to three years. When it does happen, this moon brings such opportunity and

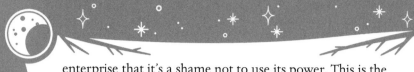

enterprise that it's a shame not to use its power. This is the moon of dreams becoming a reality. If there is something you have always wanted to do, this moon is bringing that opportunity, and you must go for it.

Black Moon Water Protection Spell
Moon Phase: Any of the black moon descriptors
Need: Jar with lid, garden soil, incense ash, ground charcoal, water

Black moon water is a powerful addition to anyone's magic collection due to not only the rarity of the event, but to the energies it brings in. Black moon water is quite easy to make, although a bit finnicky.

Fill a jar with a screw lid with tap water and add some dirt or soil from the garden, some used incense, and ground charcoal. Screw the lid tightly on and give a really good shake until the water goes black. During the night of the black moon, place on a window ledge or outside and say over the jar with your hands raised to the night sky,

> *Hear me, Goddess, I beseech,*
> *This water blesses with your power.*
> *Grace with your energies of far reach,*
> *Opportunity and protection for every hour.*

Leave out all night. In the morning, strain the water and sieve, removing all the bits of soil and so on. I usually use a coffee filter and then just throw it away or bury it deep in the garden. After you have filtered, pour into a glass bottle, label, and store the bottle in your magic cupboard or box.

Use for all manner of spells, from protection to opportunities and taking a chance on something. This black water now has the black moon's energies encased within it, and even if the black moon is not available for the next three years, you can use this water to the same desired effect.

Red Moon

Correspondences: Sex, passion, desire, menstruation

The red moon is a moon of such power, intensity, and potency that people have often feared it. The moon can appear red at times, usually around the time of the eclipse,

which many peoples feared—some even to this day refuse to go outside when there is an eclipse. However, the red moon can occur at other times and gives a subtle glow of a reddish hue. This moon packs a punch in areas to do with our inner passions, sex, and lust, but it is also the moon when many women experience a difficult time with their menstruation, especially if they have just started their periods and their body is beginning to sort its natural rhythms.

Red Moon Menstruation Spell

Moon Phase: Full Moon
Need: Moon journal

It is very difficult to write a book about the moon and her power over the earth without discussing menstruation as many of our founding beliefs stem from the connection between a woman's monthly cycle and the moon. Indeed, our very language is influenced by this connective belief, which can be traced to the beginnings of human society.

The divine feminine and the ancient Mother goddess symbolism is littered with knowledge and understanding of

menstruation, and this all points toward the moon and her almost-twenty-eight-day cycle.[42]

On the night of a red moon, begin your journey of awareness concerning the relationship between the moon and your cycles. In your moon journal, start to keep a record of when your period begins and ends. As you begin on the first night, say these words over your journal:

> *For twenty-eight days I will keep,*
> *Records of how I feel and sleep.*
> *Ancient Mother, I hear you now.*
> *Tell me your wisdom and show me how,*
> *To live in balance from month to month,*
> *To guide and help me plan in front.*

For twenty-eight days, keep the record. Write in bullet points how you feel, how you slept, and what you ate. If you suffer from migraines, headaches, aching muscles, or joints, write everything down. Include any strange dreams or experiences of déjà vu or premonitions or feelings. In your moon journal or moon chart, look at the phases of the

---

42. Miranda Gray, *Red Moon* (London: Fastprint Gold, 2009).

moon and see if you can find any patterns emerging. Use these to plan for future events in your life, such as parties or work deadlines.

White Moon

Correspondences: Spirituality, honesty, gratitude, illumination

A pure white moon illuminating the blackness of a night sky is a beautiful sight, especially if you are lost or at sea. The moon on the water radiates a light that many a seafarer often prayed for, and it shone the way home. The powerful white moon illuminates many a dark corner, and if someone has secrets, this moon can shed its light on them. The white moon can also refer to the bright crescent of a new moon, which gives the opportunity of performing these spells twice in a month if needed.

White Moon Shine Your Light Illumination Spell
Moon Phase: New Moon
Need: Moon salt, tray, white tealight candle

Illumination is a wonderful thing, especially if you've been in the dark about something for so long. If there is something you know is hidden from you, such as a family secret or a secret at work, and you feel it is time to bring it to light, perform a white moon spell on the new moon of that month. By the month's end, the full moon will shine its light and expose the darkness.

On the first night of a new moon, sprinkle some moon salt on a table or tray and write the place where the secret is—for example, office, home, family—in the salt with your index finger. Then cast this spell after lighting a white candle:

I want to know what's going on.
I want the knowledge to show,
Everything that's been happening from now on.
Shine your light upon the secrets around me.
Illuminate the darkness and bring forth into reality.
From New to Full, White Moon power, shine your luminosity.

Visualise whatever the secret might be coming into the light as a bright white moon beams onto a dark area, such as a box or corner. Imagine the box then springing open,

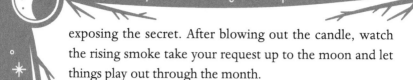

exposing the secret. After blowing out the candle, watch the rising smoke take your request up to the moon and let things play out through the month.

Yellow Moon

Correspondences: Vitality, communication, luck, chance

The yellow moon is one of those moons that brings such a presence with it, and when you see the yellow moon, it's never forgotten. The yellow moon is often depicted by artists and painters, especially the Impressionists—in particular, Vincent van Gogh and his iconic *Starry Night* painting, in which the moon is varying shades of yellow and dominating the brilliant blue night sky.

The yellow moon bursts with happiness and vitality. It is a moon that brings strength to any situation you are in, and it is a very lucky moon that can signify a windfall, so next time you see a yellow moon, buy a lottery ticket.

Yellow Moon Vitality Spell
Moon Phase: Full Moon
Need: Your imagination

If you have been burning the candle at both ends and feel absolutely exhausted, embrace the yellow moon and ask her for help. We all need vitality to get things moving, including to get us out of bed.

On the night you see a yellow moon, cast a spell for vitality. If it's not too cold outside, stand barefoot on the ground and raise your arms into the night sky, forming a Y shape with the moon in the middle. Say these words:

> *Yellow Moon of vitality light,*
> *Shine my way and make it right.*
> *No more the duvet days and lifeless ways.*
> *Come on now, please shine your rays.*

Imagine yellow light flowing into you and visualise it pulsating through every molecule and gene, racing through your body down into your toes. Bask for as long as possible in the yellow moon's light, soaking up every ounce of its vitality-giving rays. Throughout the month when you are feeling your vitality and zest diminishing, try to look at the moon, no matter what phase it is at, and imagine that feeling

returning to you. Always look for the moon to bring vitality and feel that penetrating energy commencing once again.

Orange Moon

Correspondences: Warnings, creativity, physical action, balance

Orange is a powerful moon that often signifies the end of something. It also signifies an imbalance, and so through ritual and magic, we can try to rebalance harmony in our lives and in our spiritual centre.

This is a colour of creativity and physical action. The orange moon is also highly premonitory; it can highlight coming natural disasters, and so it is wise to get prepared. Make sure your earthquake, tornado, or flood emergency kits are ready and up to speed.

Protect your most prized possessions. Natural disasters rarely give warning, but at least with an orange moon, we are being told to get ready.

Orange Moon See the Warning Sign Spell

Moon Phase: Full Moon

Need: Orange tealight candle, photo of loved ones

When you see the orange moon on the horizon, light an orange candle, hold a photo of your loved ones, and say these words:

I see the Orange Moon rising.
I can feel the warning on the horizon.
Grant all within my home and heart,
Safe passage if we are apart.
Let them see the warning signs.
Let them prepare in time.

By the light of the orange moon and the orange candle, concentrate on your loved ones and try telepathically to contact them to warn them to take care and get ready. Then blow out the candle and watch the rising smoke carry your protective intentions to the moon.

HONOURING THE FULL MOON

Here, we begin our journey of honouring the full moon with three practices for each night of the full moon, beginning with a full moon ritual. Each night of the full moon has a specific emphasis, but this is something that you can decide. For example, my first night of a full moon phase is usually a gratitude and welcoming ritual, but it is entirely up to you.

Full Moon Ritual

Altar: White candle, fennel plant / seeds, lotus oil, salt, moon journal, a picture of a moonflower or a real plant—if possible, have a full moon altar outside in a specific area of your garden filled with plants that only open at night

The Ritual (First Night of Full Moon)

There are three nights of the full moon: the night before, the night of, and the night after. Each one of the three nights can be used for magic—usually the first night of the full moon is used to give thanks for all that has been in the past month. The night of the full moon is used to manifest spells and incantations, while the final night is for healing work, either for someone or for the world in general.

When performing a full moon ritual, always stand barefoot on the earth, as you need to keep grounded—although a worshipper of the moon, you are also a child of earth, and if private enough, you can choose to go skyclad (naked). Light the white candle, dab some lotus oil onto your third eye (between your eyebrows), and hold your arms up in the air, forming the Y shape. Open your ritual with these words:

> *Welcome, Lady, on this night.*
> *For three nights, shine your light.*
> *Let the great work of magic begin,*
> *Granting all I cast therein.*
> *May your power resonate,*
> *Throughout the world, spreading love not hate.*
> *I embrace all you bring,*
> *Your energies and glory illuminating.*

Stand for some time just watching the moon and looking at her. Meditate on her energies and bathe in her moonbeams. Spend as long as you want in her rays, and when you are finished, bow to her, give thanks, and safely extinguish the candle.

Power Raising Charm (Second Night of Full Moon)

Moon Phase: Full Moon

Need: Drawstring bag, fennel seed, silver moon charm, new nail, moon salt, lock of hair

The full moon is a perfect opportunity to increase a charm that raises your power and respect either at home or at work. If you are not getting the power you deserve or if someone omits your worth in a project, create this charm.

On the second night of the full moon in a small drawstring bag, place fennel seed, a tiny silver moon charm from a pendant or a shiny new nail, three pinches of moon salt or plain sea salt, and a small lock of your hair.

> *Power raising for me this night,*
> *Power charged from darkest night to daylight.*
> *My power raised for I am right,*

Grant my respect and power might.
Silver Lady, bless this charm with all your might.

Hang the charm in a place where no one will see it but in the room you most frequent (usually high up on a shelf or in a corner of the room). Let it work its magic, and if it does not seem to be working, move it to a new location, but still out of view.

Healing Potion (Third Night of Full Moon)

A healing potion is a wonderful addition to your magical store and can be used to treat all manner of things (but always see a medical practitioner first). It is ideal to brew up on the third night of a full moon as the second is usually when major spell work is done for career, creativity, confidence—basically anything at all, while the first night is generally a gratitude spell and ritual thanking the moon for all the good gifts she has sent during the month.

Moon Phase: Full Moon
Need:

2 cups water
1 cup brown sugar
3 tablespoons fennel seeds
3 tablespoons coriander seeds
3 liquorice roots
1 stem ginger, thinly sliced
1 lemon, sliced

On the third and final night of the full moon, brew up this potion by placing all ingredients into a saucepan. Boil for twenty minutes. Turn off heat and allow to cool and steep for about an hour. As it is cooling, stir deosil and say these words over the potion:

> *Healed and blessed all who take this drink.*
> *Renew the powers of all whose lips take a sip.*
> *Healing potion on this night.*
> *Full Moon power, blessed with your light.*

Leave to cool before straining, removing lemon and ginger. Some coriander and fennel seeds may get through depending on your sieve, but these only add to the potency of the potion, so do not worry. Always label and date your bottle and use within the twenty-eight days of the month. When another full moon comes around, make a fresh batch if you need to. Use the potion like a cordial and add it to drinks; in winter, it is good hot, while in summer, it's good over ice.

Seasons with the Moon

I am a firm believer that our moon appears differently in each season. Each season brings its own powers and emphasis to magic, and the moon seems to highlight this. It is not only about the different colours that appear, but the actual size, power, and energy it exudes. We can harness that energy throughout the year by not only working with the moon itself on certain nights, but also by utilizing the power of that individual season.

Each season (lasting three months) brings a new emphasis on the moon and a new power due in part to the length of time we see her, as in the spring and summer months, the sun rules the sky. In the autumn and winter months, we see the moon the longest, culminating in the longest night in December in the northern hemisphere (June in the southern hemisphere).

SPRING

The moon in spring bursts with the same amount of energy as we find in nature. Blossoms and fresh herbs are bountiful, and we can see the wonder of the moon in all her sparkling clarity. This bountiful energy of the moon in spring helps us channel that energy into jobs we may not enjoy. One of the main tasks during the moon phases in spring concerns the cleaning, cleansing, and consecration of the environment we live and work in.

Spring is a season of extremes, from snow in the beginning to searing sun in the latter months. The changes of the earth can be seen abundantly throughout nature, from spring flowers to new life—spring lambs in the fields, wildlife returning, and swallows swooping throughout the sky.

The powerful energy of this vibrant season can be harnessed for the benefit of mind, body, and soul.

Use the spring moon to reenergise your New Year resolutions, cleanse your body and home, and change direction in life.

Spring Moon Renewal New Year Resolutions Spell

Moon Phase: Any (except Waning)
Need: Yellow tealight candle, moon journal

Use the energy of the spring moon to review your New Year resolutions. If you feel they are lagging, recharge them with the power of the spring moon.

On the night of a waxing, full, or new moon, light a yellow candle, write out your resolutions, and as you review your resolutions, say,

> *Spring Moon, renew my strength in all I do.*
> *Bring action in all my goals too.*

Think about how you can complete one or two of the resolutions by the next moon phase and work in harmony

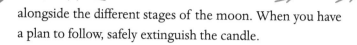

alongside the different stages of the moon. When you have a plan to follow, safely extinguish the candle.

March Harvest Moon Accept Change Spell (Southern Hemisphere)

Moon Phase: Full Moon
Need: Pictures representing the four seasons, moon journal

The world can change in an instant—as some would say, in a New York minute—and it is important to be able to adapt. At times, these sudden changes can be hard if resisted, and not everyone can be so accepting of change. If you find it difficult to be adaptable and flexible when change, either sudden or planned, comes along, try this spell.

On the March Harvest Moon, get a picture of the four seasons, such as a tree turning from spring buds to full bloom to autumn leaves and then to no leaves at all, or a seasonal garden photo. Hold both your hands over the photo and say,

> *Changing seasons, changing fast,*
> *I make plans that cannot be steadfast.*

Help me to accept the things I change,
Help me to accept the rearrange.

Sit for some time thinking about the times when you changed your ideas and plans. How did that make you feel, and what could you have done differently? Write down in your moon journal what you will do differently. When a situation arises that throws you off-kilter, do not wobble; take five deep breaths, look at that page in your journal, and remember the spell you cast. You've got this.

April Pink Moon Show Me the Money Spell (Northern Hemisphere)

Moon Phase: Full Moon
Need: Moon journal, pink pen, moon salt

On the first night of the April full moon, cast this spell to draw money to you. In your moon journal or on a piece of paper, write in pink ink the amount of money you need to get through the month. Then sprinkle moon salt over it and say,

Pink Moon of April sound,
Send this money bound.
Show me money entirely for me,
Send this money to me.

Place your right hand on the paper and visualise money finding its way to you. Leave the paper in light of the full moon. For the next two nights of the full moon phase, perform the spell exactly the same way.

May Hunter's Moon Desire Spell (Southern Hemisphere)

Moon Phase: Full Moon
Need: Bowl of water, three matches, red tealight candle

Desire is a wonderful thing—not just the physical desire of sex, but also that passion we may feel for work, a project, or an enterprise we have begun. At times, though, our desires can wane, and our enthusiasm may not be what it once was. Use the Hunter Moon of May to spring back that desire and renew your fire and passion.

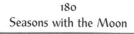

This spell can be used for anything you lost your passion and desire in, and that includes the libido. Go outside to the moon's light and, raising your hands, say,

> *You rise in the sky night after night.*
> *You shine constantly your light.*
> *Always wax, always wane.*
> *All throughout the month's pain.*
> *Am I wrong or am I right?*
> *I will cast upon you this night.*
> *Grant me the object of my desires,*
> *And help me to increase my fire.*

Light three matches and drop them in water. On the final match, light a red candle and watch how quickly the flame appears. Imagine this is your desires igniting. Each time you light the match, count how long it takes to ignite, and then count how long it takes the candle to ignite. It may take three or four seconds to take effect and grow into a strong flame. Then say,

> *From one to four seconds,*
> *That's how long it takes my desires to ignite.*

From spark to flame light,
Be I wrong or be I right.
Make my desire on fire tonight.

Go about your evening. Anytime you feel your desires waning, strike three matches once more and light the red candle to reignite your desires and spell.

SUMMER

In the summer months, we tend not to see our moon as much as days are so much longer in this season. When we do see her, we need to utilise every ounce of her energy and try to harness it in magical resources we can use throughout the rest of the three months of summer.

Summer is the season we have all been waiting for, with sun, blue skies, and light evenings. Bees and flowers are busy buzzing and blooming and energy is all around. The powerful energy of this vibrant season can be harnessed for the benefit of connection—not just of mind, body, and soul, but of parties and socialising with friends and family along with revelling in nature.

Summer Moon Healing Moonstone Water Spell

Moon Phase: Full Moon

Need: Moonstone, water

The best stone to use for water healing and drawing down the power of the moon is a moonstone. This crystal is beneficial for people, animals, and plants. It is beneficial for those who suffer from migraines and headaches, especially if they are connected to PMS.

Make a moonstone elixir by washing the stone and making sure it is clean; do not use bleach or any other chemicals when cleaning crystals. Simply place the moonstone in warm water for a couple of minutes. Place the clean moonstone into drinking water and let it soak overnight in light of the summer moon. As the stone is soaking, say these words:

> *Healing energy, flow to me.*
> *Earth, Moon, and water.*
> *Healing waters always be.*
> *Fill with the moon's energy.*

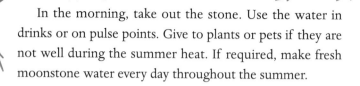

In the morning, take out the stone. Use the water in drinks or on pulse points. Give to plants or pets if they are not well during the summer heat. If required, make fresh moonstone water every day throughout the summer.

June Strawberry Moon Wedding Planner Spell (Northern Hemisphere)

Moon Phase: Full Moon
Need: Silver tealight candle

If you are apprehensive and nervous about social get-togethers, especially if you have been asked to be the best man or maid of honour and you must throw a party, including the hen-do and wedding reception, ask the moon for help.

On the Strawberry Moon, cast this spell before you embark on the wedding reception and parties. Light a silver candle and waft the light toward you with your hands. Take a few deep breaths and relax into the silver light, which represents the moon. When you are ready, say these words:

> *Let this wedding go with a swing.*
> *Let all the guests be merry and bright.*

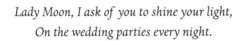

> *Lady Moon, I ask of you to shine your light,*
> *On the wedding parties every night.*

Imagine how you want the night to go and send your thoughts to the moon via the silver light of the candle. Quickly blow out the candle, enjoy the night, and when you are alone again, say thank you to the moon for a good night.

July Wolf Moon Mirror Reflection Scrying Spell (Southern Hemisphere)

Moon Phase: Full Moon
Need: Mirror, pond, bucket of water

This is an ideal spell to perform if you have a pond or even a swimming pool in your back garden. If you do not, fill a bucket with water and place the bucket under the moon so the moon's light is reflected on it. If you have a pool or pond in the garden, wait until the moon's reflection is on the water. Then, holding your mirror, carefully manoeuvre it so the moon and water are reflected back into the mirror—a sort of double reflection of moonbeams. Then look into the mirror itself and say these words:

185
Seasons with the Moon

Wolf Moon, reveal yourself to me.
Show me what only you can see.
For loved ones near and far,
Show me the past, present, and future.
Show me all what I need to see.

Keep looking as long as the moon is reflected in the water. It may start to move and shimmer and create strange shapes, but keep with it as understanding these shapes and signs is all part of learning to interpret the scrying method.

August Corn Moon Energy Zoom Spell (Northern Hemisphere)

Moon Phase: Full Moon

Need: You and a lot of determination

On the night of the August Corn Moon, cast this spell if you have a specific goal in mind that you want to achieve by the end of the month and you need all your magical energy.

Go outside on the night of the Corn Moon and, raising both your hands, say,

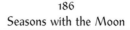

Thirty-one days I have from now,
The magical increase will wow.
In all my spells, in all I do,
Bring on the Corn Moon magic in all I view.

For the next month or thirty-one days, perform your magic every single day until you have achieved your goal. However, do not keep this level of magic up as you can become burned out and will need to take a rest. This kind of dedication is only for those times when you need to be at your optimal strength for a particular project or task. When it is over, make sure to rest completely.

AUTUMN

Autumn is probably the busiest of all the seasons due to the harvest of fields and orchards, plus school returns and many people coming back from summer holidays. For many, the autumn is indeed the season of the moon. One of the most famous magical moon festivals in this season and Halloween play a central role in defining the night sky, in particular, the very witchy full moon.

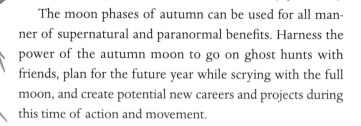

The moon phases of autumn can be used for all manner of supernatural and paranormal benefits. Harness the power of the autumn moon to go on ghost hunts with friends, plan for the future year while scrying with the full moon, and create potential new careers and projects during this time of action and movement.

Autumn Moon Ghost Hunt Spell
Moon Phase: Any (except Dark Moon)
Need: Ghost hunt event

One of the great things about autumn and all the extra energy that seems to be in the air, especially at night, is partaking in things you wouldn't do during light summer evenings. During an autumn full moon, plan a haunted night trip with your friends. There are many local events and ones that are run professionally; check out local places for alleged hauntings or join an organised ghost hunt. Before you go, make sure something doesn't attach itself to you by asking for protection from the moon.

On the night you are due to go on the ghost hunt, go outside and say to the moon, raising your arms,

Moon Goddess, I ask of you,
To protect me this night.
Shine your light and encase me too,
With your protective shield of light.
Let nothing come near to give me fright.

Visualise the moon's light encasing you in a protective silver shield and go about your evening. When performing this spell, the moon can be in any of its phases—except the dark moon. If the moon is dark, choose a different night to go. You have been warned.

September Crow Moon Magic Charm Spell (Southern Hemisphere)

Moon Phase: Full Moon
Need: Crow feathers/black feathers, white/black ribbon, autumn leaf

This is probably one of my favourite charms to make, and it becomes especially potent if you find the crow feathers yourself. Collect three black crow feathers and bind their ends together by wrapping black and white ribbon around

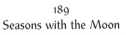

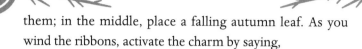

them; in the middle, place a falling autumn leaf. As you wind the ribbons, activate the charm by saying,

> *Crow Moon, I call to thee.*
> *Embracing magic is fine with me.*
> *Let all my endeavours come to be,*
> *Complete with power and purity.*
> *Success and respect in all I do,*
> *Blessed by the magic of you.*

Hang your feather charm anywhere you perform or make the most magic.

October Blood Moon Sacrifice Spell (Northern Hemisphere)

Moon Phase: Full Moon

Need: Moon water, moon journal

Habits, people, and careers can become dangerous to us if we end up sacrificing so much for them that we lose ourselves in the process. This spell can help you find yourself again.

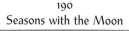

On the first night of the Blood Moon in October, sprinkle moon water in a circle around you. Standing barefoot, weather permitting, look up into the night sky and stare at the moon. Study its shape and beauty, its potential of what it will grow into, and the majesty surrounding it. Take a few deep breaths, and when you are ready, say,

I give up so much of me,
That I cannot begin to see.
Who am I or where have I been?
No more the sacrifice of myself.
From now on, I will care for myself.
October Blood Moon, let it be.
Help me to make the right choices just for me.

Stand for some time just observing the moon. When ready, go back inside and write down in your moon journal three different ways you can change your ways and life. Just write bullet points and focus on the first one, on how to instigate it and set it in motion this month.

November Flower Moon Beauty Everywhere Spell (Southern Hemisphere)

Moon Phase: Full Moon
Need: Selection of fresh flowers, bowl of water, towel, glass jar with lid

This is a lovely spell to perform at midnight or when the full Flower Moon is beaming down. Collect a selection of flowers and place them in a bowl of water. Make sure the moon is reflecting in the water. Say these words over the bowl of water:

> *Blessed waters of Flower Moon beauty,*
> *Grant me the face that only I can see.*
> *Cleansed and natural within purity.*
> *Bless this water with love and beauty.*

Splash the water over your face and wash your face in the water. Do not use any soaps or anything else, just the water. If the bowl is large enough, put your whole face in the water quickly and then dry off. Leave the water out all night underneath the Flower Moon. In the morning, bot-

tle it up in a glass jar with a lid. Each morning for the next seven days, use the Flower Moon water by adding a couple of drops to your water and washing your face with it.

WINTER

Winter is the season of the moon; our sun has almost disappeared from our skies during this cold, grey, and dark season, allowing the moon to shine more. Winter is a powerful time to harness the moon's energy for many things, including powerful hex-breaking and detoxifying spells and rituals. Use the winter to nurture, beautify, and relax, as it is indeed a healing time and a time of recollecting and remembering.

Winter Moon Memory Recall Spell

Moon Phase: Any
Need: Old family photos, photo album, pen, paper

On a winter's moonlit night, review and recollect memories. If you have old photos, create a photo album of them either digitally or in a physical book. Make sure to write the name of who is in the photo for future members of the family to

identify. If you are lucky enough to still have grandparents, take time out to sit with them one evening and create the family photo album with names, dates, and places. These are valuable times and once gone cannot be remembered.

If there is a family member's name you cannot remember or a photo you know nothing about, call upon the moon to help jog your memory.

Place the photo in the moonlight on a window ledge or somewhere in full view of the moon. Place your right hand on the photo and look straight at the moon. Say these words:

> *Lady of the Moon, help me please.*
> *Let me remember with ease.*
> *Show me in my hours of sleep,*
> *Those I meet with names complete.*

Go to bed. Keep a pen and paper next to your bed as you may be half asleep when the name pops into your head; be sure to write the names down straight away.

December Long Nights Moon Gather Round Friends Spell (Northern Hemisphere)

Moon Phase: Full Moon

Need: White tealight candle, old Christmas cards, photos of the past

The December Long Nights Moon was a chance to remember family and friends who have passed over or whom we have not seen for a long time. This tradition harks back to a time when the world was very much different, and it is often a good idea to acknowledge the past and offer remembrance to those who have gone before. This process of remembering the past is good for healing and then setting a positive intent for the future.

On the Long Nights Moon, light a white candle. Have an image or photo from the past, such as an old Christmas card from friends on your altar or table. As you light the candle, say,

Let this night be offered in remembrance of those of the past.
Let this night be in remembrance of things that could not last.

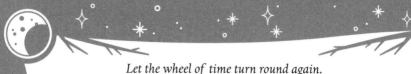

Let the wheel of time turn round again.
Let our futures be free from pain.
Gather round friends, gather round loved ones.
May our journeys together never end.
Moon of a winter's long night,
Bless us all on this very fine night.

Sit for some time remembering the past. Remember your own past, then think about how you would like the future to look. Have you learned from past mistakes? When you are ready, blow out the candle and let the rising smoke carry your intent up to the moon and universe.

January Thunder Moon Embrace the Power Spell (Southern Hemisphere)

Moon Phase: Full Moon
Need: You

The energy that builds up before something happens is quite powerful. Indeed, you may be able to sense it or feel it with goose bumps appearing on your skin, or the fine hairs at the back of your neck tingle; you may even smell the

electricity and energy in the air brewing up before a storm. Utilise this energy on the full moon and cast a spell that harnesses that power. On the night of the Thunder Moon, go outside, stand barefoot, and raise your arms to the moon, forming a Y shape, and say,

I call to thee, Lady Moon, I call to thee.
Send the power and the energy.
I embrace it all for a month long.
I harness this power and become strong.

Feel the energy flowing to you from the moon. Listen to the night and smell the air, noticing the energy all around and flowing through and from you. Stay for some time in the moonlight, embracing the extra power and energy.

February Snow Moon Family Protection Spell (Northern Hemisphere)

Moon Phase: Full Moon
Need: Pine needles, paper, pen

The cold winter weather surrounds us, and we brave the days as biting north winds bring snow and ice. At this time,

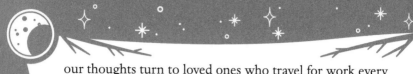

our thoughts turn to loved ones who travel for work every day or who may live far away from us. Send protection to keep them safe on cold winter days and nights. Write the name of the person you want to send protection to on a piece of white paper and scatter some pine needles over the name. Slowly roll up, making sure the pine needles do not come loose. Say these words:

Encased are you with my love,
Protected are you from above.
Winds of the north shall not touch you,
Nor shall the snows do harm.
Protected with power for every day,
In every hour and in every way.

Keep the paper in a safe place for the rest of the winter until the spring comes, then give thanks and either bury the paper in the garden or burn it and safely dispose of it.

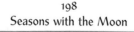

Sabbats and the Moon

The moon has been a central point in our lives. In the beginning, many if not all civilizations followed the lunar calendar. Today, two of the world's most common religions are still governed by that lunar calendar: Judaism and Islam. Moreover, three of the biggest festivals of the year are lunar festivals, with the Christian festival of Easter, Chinese New Year, and the autumn moon festival all being celebrated around the world by billions of people.

The eight festivals of the Pagan Wheel of the Year can amplify magical practices in all the phases of the moon.

During these festivals, the community celebrated the moon and seasonal changes with nighttime bonfires. Many of these traditions found their way into stories and legends such as Mischief Night, or Midsummer Eve, or May Eve— the night before the festival day was always party time as the moon was held responsible for the wild antics that would occur. The new year for many Pagans begins at Samhain, which is October 31.

SAMHAIN

Samhain, better known as Halloween, is probably the most stereotypical of all the festivals in which the moon is represented. The full moon with images of werewolves, vampires, and witches flying over it is encased in our psyche from film and television, not to mention the many different types of Halloween merchandise that represent all things moon.[43]

43. Heather Greene, *Lights, Camera, Witchcraft: A Critical History of Witches in American Film and Television* (Woodbury, MN: Llewellyn Publications, 2021).

However, Samhain is not just about witches flying on broomsticks on a full moon night; it is an incredibly important festival that marks the passing of seasons. Samhain on October 31 represents summer's end or the harvest festival. It is a time of divination and seeing into the future as Samhain is also, for many, the new year. Divination was done through apple bobbing, and many spells at this time involve the apple, probably as they were in abundance, as well as nutshells, which were burned and the ashes used to make prophecies.

Samhain Moon See the Ancestors Spell

Moon Phase: Full Moon

Need: Family photos, mirror, dragon's blood or myrrh incense, three candles (either tealight or tapered candles if in a candelabra)

Samhain has so many customs and beliefs surrounding finding love, and many view it as the festival of the dead. It is also the festival of remembering ancestors, and many cultures visit graveyards and take care of their loved ones' graves.

On Samhain and preferably when the moon is full, perform this spell to contact your ancestors. You can perform this spell at other moon phases, but not during a dark moon; it is far too dangerous due to the negative entities that are around during this time of year and the moon phase itself. This spell is not for the fainthearted, so if you are easily scared, please do not perform this spell.

Place photos of your ancestors around your dinner table. If you do not have any photos of them, write their names out and place them on the table as place cards. In the centre of the table, have a candelabra or three candles that represent past, present, and future.

Next to you, have a mirror or your phone—something with a reflective surface—and burn some dragon's blood or myrrh incense. Make sure all the lights are turned off and you will not be disturbed; only the light from the candles should illuminate the room along with the moon if she is full. Place both your hands on the table, palms facing down; take a few deep breaths and say,

> *Moon of Dark, which beams the light,*
> *Bring forth my ancestors this night.*

Open up the veil and let me see,
The faces of ancestors and family.
I call to thee; I call to thee.
Release them now and set them free.
Enter here upon this night,
Shed your beams with guiding light.

If the candles begin to flicker or go out, this is a sign your ancestors have arrived. The incense may also waft a different direction as if someone had just walked past it. Then, taking the mirror in your hands, turn around to look at your ancestors through the mirror with your back to them; look into the reflection over your shoulder. Commune with your ancestors and enjoy the evening. When it is time to say goodbye, you must close the spell and make sure they return from whence they came.

Let the incense burn out and then say,

Blessed Goddess of the Moon,
Your light doth shine this night.
Thank you to my family and my ancestors.
It was good to behold your sights.

But now you must return, and the veil will close.
No more the pain and the sorrows,
For I am blessed that you were here.
See you again, same place next year.

Blow out the candles and visualise the rising smoke taking your ancestors up to heaven.

YULE

Yule is the festival that follows the ancient Midwinter solstice and can last anywhere from the entire month of December to, more traditionally, twelve days, from which we get the twelve days of Christmas. As the winter solstice falls within this month, the moon shines the longest in our skies now, and we can perform much magic underneath her watchful gaze.

This is the time of year when candles light the way and social gatherings and parties with friends and family are in full swing. It is also a time when we can capitalise on the power of the moon to perform not only fertility magic, but also recovery spells of long-lost objects; December is the final month of the year, and this is the last chance to find lost things.

Yule Moon Return to Me Once Again Spell

Moon Phase: Full Moon

Need: Pen, paper, fireproof container, white tealight candle

The Yule moon is a good time to recall something that is lost to you, such as a pet or an item of jewellery that, although you have searched for it all year, simply has not reappeared. You cannot perform this spell for a lost love, as imposing your will on someone else is likely to backfire with disastrous results.

On the full moon during the time of Yule, call for your lost item. Write the name or what you have lost on a piece of paper, then roll it up like a scroll. Light a white candle and, holding the scroll in your right hand, say these words:

> *Yule, return to me once again.*
> *Yule Moon, feel my pain.*
> *Return to me that which is lost,*
> *Safe and sound and at no cost.*

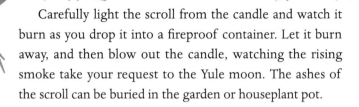

Carefully light the scroll from the candle and watch it burn as you drop it into a fireproof container. Let it burn away, and then blow out the candle, watching the rising smoke take your request to the Yule moon. The ashes of the scroll can be buried in the garden or houseplant pot.

IMBOLC

Although at Imbolc the sun is beginning to return and our nights are getting shorter, we can still see the moon in all her wonderous power. The Imbolc full moon is an enigmatic one, especially if there is snow on the ground; her moonbeams upon the white landscape seem to skip with expectant magic. Imbolc moon spells embrace the Goddess and the emerging spring as winter begins to creep back once more into total darkness. In other traditions, Imbolc is called Candlemas, or Saint Brigid's Day, or Groundhog Day. The Festival of Lights, as Imbolc is also called, is regarded as the first stirrings of spring, with the first flowers, such as snowdrops and crocus, beginning to show their delicate heads.

Imbolc Moon Triple Goddess Spell

Moon Phases: Any (New Moon is ideal)
Need: Goddess representation in her maiden form

Throughout the festivals of the year, the Goddess waxes and wanes just as everything in our universe, and in the Triple Goddess tradition, the winter is regarded as the Crone. Come Imbolc, she is reborn as the Maiden.

On Imbolc and underneath the moon (hopefully the new moon), embrace the Goddess and feel renewed. On your altar or outside underneath the night sky, perform this spell. Raise your hands to the moon and say,

> *Goddess of the New Moon,*
> *You emerge from the old into the new.*
> *Your gifts of innocence and wonder bring*
> *All the potential of the Spring.*
> *I embrace the Maiden Goddess of the new,*
> *And give gratitude to the Crone of Winter past,*
> *As the Mother of Summer will come at last.*

On your altar or in a special place, have a representation of the Goddess in her Maiden form.

OSTARA

Ostara is the first festival of the spring and signifies the warmth returning to the earth once more. In some circles traditionally, this is the time when we plant the seeds that will be gathered at the last harvest. Nowadays, it all depends on the weather!

The Ostara moon brings with it extra power of protection and energy in all endeavours, but more importantly, this moon brings so much luck, and any activities or careers beginning during this time will bring success. There is new life everywhere, and so the egg has become a symbol of Ostara. Decorate your altar with spring flowers, such as daffodils and narcissi.

Ostara Moon Hare Lucky Charm Spell

Moon Phase: Any
Need: Silver hare charm, yellow tealight candle

The hare is a symbol of the spring and accompanies the goddess Eostre. Hares are nocturnal animals and tend to feed at night as they mainly rest during the day. They have been symbols of luck for centuries and represent the spring moon in all her phases. You can get many little hare charms from online stores or at your local jewellery shop. Always buy a silver hare if you are working with moon magic as silver is the metal of the moon.

On Ostara night during a waxing, new, or full moon, light a yellow candle and carefully waft your hare charm through its light. Say,

> *Ostara light, moon bright,*
> *Grant this hare good luck tonight.*
> *For now, and evermore,*
> *Let this hare bring success and more.*

Depending on where you want and need luck—whether at home or work, with finances or love—keep your little hare charm with you on your purse, wallet, or keychain, and carry it with you for the rest of the year.

BELTANE

Beltane, the Festival of Fire, is a powerful time of the year. It is a highly charged and extremely potent festival, and the night before May Day is often celebrated the most. Traditionally,

it began at sunset on April 30 and lasted until May Day. This day has long been a celebration of fertility and dancing, notably around the maypole. May Day is a wonderful festival.

Beltane is sometimes known as the Fire Festival due to the bonfires that are lit at night. It is also the spring festival of merrymaking. At Beltane, like Halloween, it is said that witches, fairies, and ghosts wander freely. The veil between the worlds is thin. There are lots of myths about this night, and one of them concerns the full moon and the Fairy Queen. Folklore says that if you sit beneath a tree on a full moon this night, you will see or hear the Fairy Queen and the bells on her horse. If you hide your face, she will pass you by, but if you look at her, she will choose you!

Beltane Moon Ribbon Charm
Moon Phase: Any but Dark or Waning
Need: Red and white ribbons of equal length

On the night of the Beltane moon, which can be in any of her phases except dark or waning, create a ribbon charm for not only your own fertility, but also to represent the earth in all her fruitfulness.

Have two ribbons of equal length, one red and one white, as they represent the bonding of male and female, which in turn symbolises the Lord of the Greenwood and the Queen of May. In other traditions, this charm symbolised the dance of the year between the sun and the moon. Weave the two ribbons together to create a rope pattern. As you do, say these words:

> *Weave these ribbons of time and place.*
> *Sun and Moon dance through space.*
> *Beltane Moon, bless all with your grace,*
> *Upon those you shine, with health*
> *and happiness throughout the year,*
> *Wherever they may be, whether they are far or near.*

Tie the ends together and leave in the moonlight on Beltane night. In the morning, hang the charm up. You can also make little ribbon bracelets and charge them in the moonlight on Beltane as gifts of protection for your friends.

LITHA/MIDSUMMER

For many people, Litha or Midsummer is the highlight of the year, especially Midsummer Eve, which has traditionally been a time of much magic and merrymaking when the entire night was spent dancing underneath the moon. Midsummer is the time of the mystical and elemental power of the Goddess, with legends and myths of fairies, goblins, and all manner of nature spirits interacting with humans. The moon in all these legends plays a key role in the antics these mischievous entities get up to.

The summer solstice is when the sun is at its height. It is the longest day of the year, and poets and playwrights the world over have written about the magic of Midsummer. It is said that a child conceived on Midsummer is spiritually blessed. This is interesting, as a child conceived on Midsummer is likely to be a Pisces, and they are renowned for being highly spiritual and in touch with other realms.

Midsummer Moon Litha Wand Spell
Moon Phase: Ideally Full Moon or New Moon

Need: Selection of available herbs, flowers, crystals; silver ribbon

There is nothing better than making a fairy moonlight wand on Midsummer, and they are surprisingly easy to make. You can either make a larger one for yourself or a smaller one especially for the fairies; leave it out on Midsummer Eve and ask the fairies to sprinkle some dust on it for extra power.

I prefer to make fairy wands out of herbs, such as a rosemary branch with lavender with daisies and jewels tied together with silver ribbon. You can use any type of herb or flower you are growing or like at this time of year.

Try to make the wand outside underneath the Midsummer moon. As you wrap the ribbon and herbs around your wand, cast this spell upon it:

Midsummer Moon, hear my plea.
I am making this for thee.
I ask that you grace this gift,
With magic and power from your silvery light,
Especially blessed by those with fairy flight.

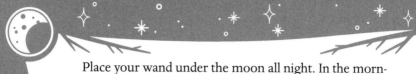

Place your wand under the moon all night. In the morning, use inside the house, place on your altar, take to work to bring a bit of extra magic, or leave outside for the magic of your garden to grow better.

LAMMAS

Lammas is the first festival of the harvest and signifies the turning of the wheel. It's a festival tinged with sadness that days are getting shorter, and summer is gradually ending. Lammas is usually represented by wheat, so loaves of bread, corn dollies, and sunflowers, which are also out in abundance in August, all represent this festival. There is a tradition that if couples suspected the fairies of snatching their child on May Day and replacing it with a changeling child, the process could be reversed at Lammas. The full moon at Lammas can often appear yellow or orange as if the Goddess already feels the turning of the wheel on earth and accommodates her colours. The magic contained within this moon is all about gratitude and respect.

Lammas Moon Bread Spell

Moon Phase: Preferably Full Moon or New Moon

Need:

500 grams bread flour

1 teaspoon salt

1 teaspoon sea salt

25 grams / 1 ounce fresh yeast or 1 packet yeast made up to
   specifications

3 tablespoons olive oil

300 millilitres warm water

Flavourings such as rosemary, honey, sunflower seeds—any
   of the symbols of Lammas

Moon salt and extra herbs for sprinkling (optional)

Try your hand baking this bread or, failing that, buy a freshly baked loaf on Lammas. Moon bread is basically a round, fluffy focaccia with the dimpled appearance of moon craters. This is actually a very fun activity to do and the easiest type of bread to make.

Place the flour, salts, yeast, water, and oil in a bowl and mix until it makes a soft, sticky dough. Lightly oil the work

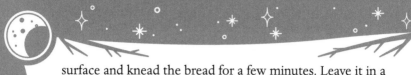

surface and knead the bread for a few minutes. Leave it in a larger bowl and cover it. When it has doubled in size, knead it again. Halve the dough and knead in your chosen flavouring. For honey, just drizzle a tablespoon of it into the mixture and make sure it's kneaded well. Say these words as you knead:

> *Blessings to you, Moon of Lammas.*
> *The Wheel has turned at last.*
> *I thank you for the summer past.*
> *I welcome all the magic of the autumn moons,*
> *And embrace the coming winter soon.*

Place on a baking sheet and work into a round moonlike shape. Press your index finger into it to create moon craters. Cover once more and leave for a further thirty minutes to rise again. After, drizzle generously with olive oil and sprinkle some moon salt and extra herbs over it if desired. Bake in a preheated oven for twenty minutes at 390°F (200°C). You can add any additional Lammas fruits, herbs, or flowers to the moon bread, such as pears, myrtle, barley, rice, basil, mint, rosemary, and sunflower.

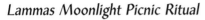

Lammas Moonlight Picnic Ritual

Moon Phase: Any (Full Moon is ideal)

Need: Selection of picnic food, mead or honeyed wine, Lammas bread

There is something so magical about having a moonlit picnic on Lammas as it is probably the last picnic of the year if you live in a cold climate (although, as someone who does enjoy a picnic in a snowy forest with a -15°C temperature, eating outside can be enjoyable all year). In your Lammas picnic, make sure to have your moon bread and plenty of early fruits, such as raspberries and plums. It is also traditional to drink mead at this time or at least have honey represented in some form. Have a glass of mead or honeyed wine, raise your glass to the moon, and say,

> *Glory to the Moon on high.*
> *I thank you for your many gifts the summer doth bring,*
> *And I honour you with all my honour and power.*
> *Thank you for your gracious light,*
> *That has shone for these summer nights.*

Blessed be to you, Lady,
And may you shine forevermore on me.

While enjoying the moonlight picnic, write in your moon journal what you are grateful for this summer. Have you finished a project, taken exams, found new love, or moved house? Write down what you are thankful for. After you have eaten, lie back on your picnic blanket and gaze at the moon, studying all her features, sending your gratitude for her overseeing power in everything you do.

MABON

Mabon is the second harvest festival and the start of winter preparations; it's a time of contemplation, so take time out and use it as a beauty day. The moon at Mabon is powerful in all her phases, especially dark or waning—there may be things you want the waning Mabon moon to take away from you, such as a negative period or a bad relationship. It is traditionally a good time to enact rituals for protection and security, so you could try a money spell or a career enhancement spell.

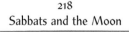

Mabon Moon Embrace the Encroaching Dark Spell

Moon Phase: Any

Need: Rose hips, apples, sage, a black tealight candle, a white tealight candle

After the long nights of summer, there is something wonderful about the dark nights, and my Lady Moon finally takes ownership of the sky once more. Do not fear the dark or the nights; acknowledge them and revel in the power they bring, as there is so much potential for creativity and learning within the early nights of the year. We are no longer distracted by the sunshine and being outdoors all the time.

On Mabon's moon, place rose hips, apples, and sage on your altar and light one black and one white candle. Take an apple in your hands and say these words:

> *Come the dark, come the night.*
> *Goddess of the Moon, return and shine your light.*
> *The dark nights are approaching,*
> *As winter is encroaching.*
> *Welcome to the Moon, this autumn night.*
> *I will embrace the dark without fright.*

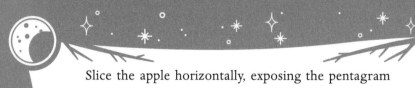

Slice the apple horizontally, exposing the pentagram inside, and leave the two halves on your altar for the rest of the month. As they dry out and decay, the nights will become considerably darker, and your fear of the dark night will lessen.

Moon in Magic

Alas, we have come to the end of our moon journey, and I hope I have given you many ideas for working in harmony with our Lady of the Night. She graces our lives in so many ways that we can take her for granted. Yet her presence has found its way into every part of our human existence, from art to culture to religion to our lunar calendars to the festivals that honour her in all her phases. The moon has helped us make sense of the world and has soothed troubled souls. Around the world, people still raise their arms to her in reverence and splendour while performing rituals in her honour.

There is so much energy contained within the moon in all her many cycles that power and potential are available to us each night; all we need to do is look up and ask. I have

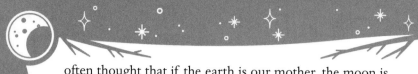

often thought that if the earth is our mother, the moon is our cool aunt whom, even though we may not see her, we know is there for us always, and we just have to ask her for anything.

While Mother Earth can be a bit of a disciplinarian when she wants to dish out punishment (tornados, earthquakes, floods), our Auntie Moon is reliable and dependable and does not chastise us. We can use her phases for absolutely everything in our lives, and her power is constant, never fading, and always certain. The moon will be there long after we have left this planet, but she will always be part of us, no matter where we are in the universe.

Spell Appendix

Protection

Resolutions

Ritual

Moon Correspondence Chart

Moon Phase	Colours	Oils	Herbs	Plants
Full Moon	White	Lotus	Fennel	Moon Flower
Dark Moon	Black	Patchouli	Belladonna	Black Tulip
Waning	Green	Cedar	Mint	Ivy
Waxing	Red	Rose	Rosemary	Dianthus
New Moon	Yellow	Lemon	Dill	Daffodil
Gibbous	Blue	Lavender	Hyssop	Morning Glory

Moon Months

NORTHERN AND SOUTHERN
HEMISPHERE CHART

For a quick reference, a chart of all the moon's phases and
their months is provided on the next page.

Month	Northern Hemisphere	Southern Hemisphere	Emphasis
January	Wolf Moon	Thunder Moon	Reflection / Power
February	Snow Moon	Corn Moon	Family / Energy
March	Crow Moon	Harvest Moon	Magic / Change
April	Pink Moon	Blood Moon	Finances / Sacrifice
May	Flower Moon	Hunter's Moon	Beauty / Desire
June	Strawberry Moon	Long Nights Moon	Marriage / Friends
July	Thunder Moon	Wolf Moon	Power / Reflection
August	Corn Moon	Snow Moon	Energy / Family
September	Harvest Moon	Crow Moon	Change / Magic
October	Blood Moon	Pink Moon	Sacrifice / Finances
November	Hunter's Moon	Flower Moon	Desire / Beauty
December	Long Nights Moon	Strawberry Moon	Friends / Marriage

References

Binney, Ruth. *Wise Words & Country Ways: Weather Lore.*
Devon, UK: David & Charles, 2010.

Charles, R. H., trans. *The Book of Enoch.* Missouri: Defender
Publisher, 2016.

Coredon, Christopher. *A Dictionary of Medieval Terms and
Phrases.* Woodbridge: D. S. Brewer Publishers, 2007.

Davidson, Gustav. *A Dictionary of Angels.* London: Free
Press, 1994.

Day, Brian. *A Chronicle of Folk Customs.* London: Octopus
Publishing Group, 1998.

Eason, Cassandra. *The New Crystal Bible.* London: Carlton
Books, 2010.

Forty, Jo. *Classic Mythology.* London: Grange Books, 1999.

Gray, Miranda. *Red Moon.* London: Fastprint Gold, 2009.

Green, C. M. C. *Roman Religion and the Cult of Diana at Aricia.* New York: Cambridge University Press, 2007.

Greene, Heather. *Lights, Camera, Witchcraft: A Critical History of Witches in American Film and Television.* Woodbury, MN: Llewellyn Publications, 2021.

Harding, Mike. *A Little Book of The Green Man.* London: Aurum Press, 1998.

Kollerstrom, Nick. *Gardening & Planting by the Moon.* Marlow: Foulsham, 2023.

Leland, C. G. *Aradia, or the Gospel of Witches.* London: David Butt, 1899.

Mathews, John. *The Quest for the Green Man.* Wheaton: Quest Books, 2001.

McCrae, Niall. *The Moon and Madness.* London: Imprint Academic, 2011.

Moorey, Teresa. *The Fairy Bible.* London: Octopus Publishing Group, 2008.

O'Rush, Claire. *The Enchanted Garden*. London: Random House, 2000.

Palmer, Martin, and Nigel Palmer. *Sacred Britain: A Guide to the Sacred Sites and Pilgrim Routes of England, Scotland and Wales*. London: Piatkus, 1997.

Radin, Dean. *Real Magic: Ancient Wisdom, Modern Science, and a Guide to the Secret Power of the Universe*. Listening Library, 2018.

Stroud, Rick. *The Book of the Moon*. London: Doubleday, 2009.

Tudorbeth. *The Hedgewitch's Little Book of Flower Magic*. Woodbury, MN: Llewellyn Publications, 2023.

———. *The Hedgewitch's Little Book of Seasons*. Woodbury, MN: Llewellyn Publications, 2022.

———. *The Hedgewitch's Little Book of Spells, Charms & Brews*. Woodbury, MN: Llewellyn Publications, 2021.

Waite, Arthur Edward. *The Book of Ceremonial Magic: Including the Rites and Mysteries of Goetic Theurgy, Sorcery, and Infernal Necromancy*. Connecticut: Martino Fine Books, 2011. Reprint.

TO WRITE TO THE AUTHOR

If you wish to contact the author or would like more information about this book, please write to the author in care of Llewellyn Worldwide Ltd. and we will forward your request. Both the author and the publisher appreciate hearing from you and learning of your enjoyment of this book and how it has helped you. Llewellyn Worldwide Ltd. cannot guarantee that every letter written to the author can be answered, but all will be forwarded. Please write to:

Tudorbeth
℅ Llewellyn Worldwide
2143 Wooddale Drive
Woodbury, MN 55125-2989

Please enclose a self-addressed stamped envelope for reply,
or $1.00 to cover costs. If outside the U.S.A., enclose
an international postal reply coupon.

Many of Llewellyn's authors have websites with additional information and resources. For more information, please visit our website at http://www.llewellyn.com.